MACHINE LEARNING ALGORITHMS: HANDBOOK

A STEP-BY-STEP GUIDE TO ALL MACHINE LEARNING ALGORITHMS WITH IMPLEMENTATION USING PYTHON!

Aman Kharwal

Chennai • Bangalore

CLEVER FOX PUBLISHING
Chennai, India

Published by CLEVER FOX PUBLISHING 2023
Copyright © Aman Kharwal 2023

All Rights Reserved.
ISBN: 978-93-56484-83-2

This book has been published with all reasonable efforts taken to make the material error-free after the consent of the author. No part of this book shall be used, reproduced in any manner whatsoever without written permission from the author, except in the case of brief quotations embodied in critical articles and reviews.

The Author of this book is solely responsible and liable for its content including but not limited to the views, representations, descriptions, statements, information, opinions and references ["Content"]. The Content of this book shall not constitute or be construed or deemed to reflect the opinion or expression of the Publisher or Editor. Neither the Publisher nor Editor endorse or approve the Content of this book or guarantee the reliability, accuracy or completeness of the Content published herein and do not make any representations or warranties of any kind, express or implied, including but not limited to the implied warranties of merchantability, fitness for a particular purpose. The Publisher and Editor shall not be liable whatsoever for any errors, omissions, whether such errors or omissions result from negligence, accident, or any other cause or claims for loss or damages of any kind, including without limitation, indirect or consequential loss or damage arising out of use, inability to use, or about the reliability, accuracy or sufficiency of the information contained in this book.

Index

Index	1
Overview	5
Key Features:	5
About the Author	7
Preparing a Python Virtual Environment for Machine Learning	**8**
Creating a Python Virtual Environment:	8
Chapter 1: Machine Learning Algorithms: An Overview	**11**
Types of Machine Learning Algorithms	13
And Finally, The Machine Learning Techniques	15
Summary	16
Chapter 2: Getting Started with Regression Algorithms	**18**
Linear Regression	19
Introduction	19
Implementation of Linear Regression	20
Advantages & Disadvantages of Linear Regression	23
Multiple Regression	24
Introduction	24
Polynomial Regression	25
Introduction	25
Implementation of Polynomial Regression	27
Advantages & Disadvantages of Polynomial Regression	29
Ridge Regression	29
Introduction	29
Implementation of Ridge Regression	30
Advantages & Disadvantages of Ridge Regression	32
Lasso Regression	33
Introduction	33
Implementation of Lasso Regression	34
Advantages & Disadvantages of Lasso Regression	36
Elastic Net Regression	37
Introduction	37
Implementation of Elastic Net Regression	38
Advantages & Disadvantages of Elastic Net Regression	39
Summary	39
Chapter 3: Linear Classification Algorithms	**41**
Logistic Regression	42

Introduction..42
  Implementation of Logistic Regression..43
  Advantages & Disadvantages of Logistic Regression.......................44
  Linear Discriminant Analysis (LDA)..45
    Introduction..45
    Implementation of LDA..46
    Advantages & Disadvantages of LDA..47
  Stochastic Gradient Descent Classifier...48
    Introduction..48
    Implementation of SGD Classification Algorithm............................49
    Advantages & Disadvantages of SGD Classification Algorithm...........50
  Summary..50
Chapter 4: Performance Evaluation Methods....................................52
    Accuracy..53
    Precision..55
    Recall..56
    F1 Score...57
    Confusion Matrix...58
    AUC & ROC..60
  Regression Performance Evaluation Metrics...63
    Introduction..63
    Mean Squared Error...63
    Root Mean Squared Error...65
    Mean Absolute Error..67
    R-squared..68
    Adjusted R-squared...69
  Summary..70
Chapter 5: Naive Bayes..72
    Introduction..72
    Naive Bayes Algorithms...74
    Gaussian Naive Bayes..75
    Multinomial Naive Bayes...78
    Bernoulli Naive Bayes...80
    Advantages & Disadvantages of Naive Bayes Algorithm..............82
    Summary..83
Chapter 6: Support Vector Machines..84
    Introduction..84
    The Concept of Decision Boundary in SVM....................................85
    Implementation of SVM for Classification.......................................87
    SVM for Regression..89
    Advantages & Disadvantages of SVM...92
    Summary..92
Chapter 7: Decision Trees & Ensemble Methods...............................94
    Introduction..94
    Decision Trees Algorithms & Ensemble Methods..........................96

- The Concept of Ensemble Methods in Decision Trees ... 97
- CART ... 98
- ID3 ... 101
- C4.5 ... 103
- Random Forests ... 105
- The Concept of Bagging in Random Forests ... 107
- Implementation of Random Forests ... 109
- Gradient Boosting ... 110
- The Concept of Boosting in Gradient Boosting ... 111
- Advantages & Disadvantages of Decision Trees and Ensemble Methods ... 113
- Summary ... 114

Chapter 8: Boosting Algorithms ... 115
- Getting Started with Adaboost ... 116
- The Boosting Process ... 118
  - Weight Updates: ... 118
  - Error Minimization: ... 119
- Implementation of AdaBoost ... 120
- XGBoost (Extreme Gradient Boosting) ... 122
- Key Enhancements in XGBoost ... 123
- Implementation of XGBoost ... 124
- Summary ... 125

Chapter 9: Clustering Algorithms ... 127
- K-means ... 130
  - Implementation of K-means ... 132
  - Advantages & Disadvantages of K-means ... 134
- DBSCAN ... 135
  - Implementation of DBSCAN ... 136
  - Advantages & Disadvantages of DBSCAN ... 137
- Agglomerative Clustering ... 138
  - Implementation of Agglomerative Clustering ... 140
- BIRCH Clustering ... 142
  - Implementation of BIRCH Clustering ... 143
  - Advantages & Disadvantages of BIRCH Clustering ... 145
- Mean Shift Clustering ... 146
  - Implementation of Mean Shift Clustering ... 147
  - Advantages & Disadvantages of Mean Shift Clustering ... 148
  - Summary ... 149

Chapter 10: Important Data Preprocessing Elements To Train Better Models ... 152
- Getting Started with Handling Missing Values ... 152
- Handling Outliers ... 155
- Feature Selection ... 157
- Principal Component Analysis ... 160
- Feature Scaling ... 162
- Hyperparameter Tuning ... 165
- SMOTE ... 167

Summary 169
Chapter 11: Neural Network Architectures for Deep Learning 170
    Introduction 170
    The Computational Structure of Neural Networks 171
    How Neural Networks Work? 172
    Getting Started with Perceptron 174
    Multi-layer Perceptrons 176
    Convolutional Neural Networks 179
    Recurrent Neural Networks 182
    Long Short-Term Memory Networks 185
    Generative Adversarial Networks 188
    Transformer Networks 193
    Summary 196
Chapter 12: Exploring Time Series Forecasting Algorithms 198
    Introduction 198
    Getting Started with ARIMA for Time Series Forecasting 199
    SARIMA for Time Series Forecasting 205
    Summary 208
Appendix: All Parameters of Commonly Used Machine Learning Algorithms 209
    Linear Regression: 209
    Polynomial Regression: 210
    Ridge Regression: 210
    Lasso Regression: 211
    Elastic Net Regression: 211
    Logistic Regression: 212
    Linear Discriminant Analysis: 213
    Stochastic Gradient Descent Classifier: 214
    Naive Bayes: 215
    Support Vector Machines: 216
    Decision Trees: 217
    Random Forests: 219
    Gradient Boosting: 220
    K-Means: 222
    DBSCAN: 224
    Convolutional Neural Networks: 225
    Recurrent Neural Networks: 227
Final Words - From the Author 228

Overview

In "Machine Learning Algorithms: Handbook", Aman Kharwal, founder of Statso.io, takes you on an enlightening journey through the fascinating world of machine learning. Whether you are a seasoned data scientist or a curious beginner, this book provides a holistic overview of the essential algorithms that form the backbone of modern machine learning.

With clarity and precision, Aman demystifies complex concepts, guiding you step-by-step through the fundamentals of regression, classification, clustering, deep learning, and time series forecasting. Each chapter presents a deep dive into a specific algorithm, equipping you with the knowledge and skills to tackle real-world problems head-on.

Key Features:

1. **Clear Explanations of Machine Learning Algorithms:** The book offers clear and concise explanations of machine learning algorithms, ensuring that readers of all levels can grasp the concepts effortlessly.
2. **Hands-On Approach:** Packed with practical examples using Python and code snippets, you'll gain a hands-on understanding of how each algorithm works and learn to implement them in real projects.
3. **Comprehensive Coverage:** From linear regression and support vector machines to decision trees and neural networks, the book covers a wide array of algorithms, giving you a solid foundation to explore diverse problem domains.
4. **Performance Evaluation Methods:** Learn how to evaluate the effectiveness of your models, identify areas for improvement, and optimize their performance using industry-standard evaluation techniques.

5. **Data Preprocessing Techniques:** Discover the critical elements of data preprocessing that lay the groundwork for building robust and accurate machine learning models.
6. **Time Series Forecasting:** Explore advanced algorithms specifically designed for time series data, a critical component of numerous real-world applications.
7. **Appendix for Easy Reference:** Access all parameters of commonly used machine learning algorithms in a handy appendix, facilitating efficient model tuning.

Whether you are interested in learning the fundamentals of all Machine Learning algorithms, implementation of Machine Learning algorithms using Python, or preparing for an interview, "Machine Learning Algorithms: Handbook" will help you in every way.

About the Author

Aman Kharwal is a highly regarded Data Strategist, entrepreneur, and contributor in the Data Science field with a passion for demystifying complex topics in the field of data science and machine learning. As the founder of Statso.io, a thriving data science community, he has helped countless individuals and businesses leverage the power of data to drive informed decisions. Aman's dedication to making machine learning accessible to all shines through in this comprehensive and approachable handbook.

Having made the transition from a business and finance background, Aman's deep passion for using data to solve business problems has led him to become one of the most sought-after experts in the field. Using his extensive experience and expertise, Aman has created an extensive library of content focused on leveraging machine learning algorithms to drive business success.

In his latest book, Machine Learning Algorithms: Handbook, Aman brings his wealth of knowledge and experience to the fore. Drawing on his practical knowledge, Aman provides a comprehensive guide to help readers navigate the complexities of machine learning algorithms and their applications. With this book, Aman is set to continue his legacy of shaping the data science community and empowering businesses around the world.

Preparing a Python Virtual Environment for Machine Learning

Before getting started with this book, it's highly recommended to set up a Python virtual environment for Machine Learning. Although you can use tools like Google Colab, which is completely ready to use for Machine Learning, still if you are aiming to learn Machine Learning, setting up a Python virtual environment is something you should know.

A Python virtual environment is a self-contained workspace that allows you to isolate Python projects and their dependencies from each other. It helps avoid conflicts between different project requirements and ensures that packages installed for one project do not interfere with others. This is particularly useful when working on multiple projects with different package versions or when collaborating with others.

In a Python virtual environment for Machine Learning, you typically need to install the following essential libraries and packages:

- NumPy: For numerical computations and arrays.
- Pandas: For data manipulation and analysis.
- Matplotlib, Seaborn, and Plotly: For data visualization.
- Scikit-learn: For machine learning algorithms and tools.
- TensorFlow or PyTorch: For deep learning models.

Creating a Python Virtual Environment:

To set up a Python virtual environment, follow the steps mentioned below:

- Step 1: Open Command Prompt (Terminal in case of Mac).

- Step 2: Install virtualenv by running: pip install virtualenv.

- Step 3: Navigate to the directory where you want to create the virtual environment using the cd command.

- Step 4: Create a virtual environment named "env" by running: virtualenv env.

- Step 5: Activate the virtual environment with the command: .\env\Scripts\activate.

If you are using a Mac then you have to install pip in your systems before following the above process. You can install the pip in your system by executing the command mentioned below:

curl https://bootstrap.pypa.io/get-pip.py -o get-pip.py

Once the virtual environment is activated, you can start installing the required libraries and packages using pip. Below are all the Python libraries you need to install in your virtual environment:

- pip install numpy
- pip install pandas
- pip install matplotlib
- pip install seaborn
- pip install plotly
- pip install scikit-learn
- pip install Keras
- pip install tensorflow

In case of Mac, pip install tensorflow will not work. Below are the commands that will install tensorflow in your MacOS:

- pip install tensorflow-macos
- pip install tensorflow-metal
- pip install tensorflow_datasets

Chapter 1: Machine Learning Algorithms: An Overview

Welcome to the exciting world of Machine Learning! If you're new to this field, you might be wondering what machine learning is and how it can be used to solve real-world problems.

Machine Learning is a subset of artificial intelligence (AI) that focuses on the development of algorithms and statistical models that enable computers to learn and improve their performance on a specific task without being explicitly programmed.

It involves creating mathematical models that learn from and make predictions or decisions based on data patterns. The main goal of machine learning is to allow computers to adapt and improve their performance over time by learning from new data, thus enabling them to make accurate predictions, classify objects, or optimize decisions without human intervention.

Machine learning algorithms are sets of rules and mathematical models that enable computers to learn patterns from data and make predictions or decisions based on that learning. These algorithms analyze data, identify patterns, and create mathematical representations that can be used to make predictions or solve specific problems.

There are various types of machine learning algorithms, including supervised learning (learning from labelled data), unsupervised learning (learning from unlabeled data), and reinforcement learning (learning from feedback and rewards).

Here are some examples of how machine learning algorithms can be used to solve business problems:

- **Customer Segmentation:** Machine learning algorithms can analyze customer data, such as purchase history and demographic information, to segment customers into distinct groups based on their preferences and behaviour. This segmentation can help businesses target specific customer segments with personalized marketing strategies and improve customer satisfaction.

- **Credit Risk Assessment:** Financial institutions can use machine learning algorithms to analyze historical customer data and credit scores to assess the credit risk of loan applicants. This helps in making more accurate and data-driven decisions on loan approvals and interest rates.

- **Predictive Maintenance:** Machine learning algorithms can analyze sensor data from industrial equipment to predict potential equipment failures before they occur. This enables businesses to schedule maintenance proactively, reducing downtime and minimizing operational costs.

- **Demand Forecasting:** Retailers can use machine learning algorithms to analyze historical sales data and external factors like weather and holidays to predict future demand for products accurately. This helps in optimizing inventory levels and supply chain management.

- **Natural Language Processing (NLP):** Machine learning algorithms can be used in NLP applications to analyze and understand human language. Businesses can use NLP to automate customer support through chatbots, sentiment analysis of customer feedback, and extracting valuable insights from unstructured text data.

- **Image and Speech Recognition:** Machine learning algorithms can be employed in image and speech recognition systems. Businesses can use these systems for various purposes, such as facial recognition for security applications, voice-controlled virtual assistants, and automatic image tagging for organizing large image databases.

> In short, Machine Learning means using data and algorithms to build intelligent systems that help in solving business problems.

Types of Machine Learning Algorithms

In the world of machine learning, there are three main types of algorithms: supervised learning, unsupervised learning, and reinforcement learning. Each of these types of algorithms has its own unique approach to learning from data and making predictions or decisions.

- **Supervised learning:** In supervised learning, the algorithm needs to learn from labelled data, which means the input data is already associated with known output values. The goal of the algorithm is to learn a mapping function from input to output that can be used to make predictions about new unseen data. Supervised learning algorithms can be used for tasks such as regression, classification, and prediction.

- **Unsupervised learning:** In unsupervised learning, the algorithm needs to learn from unlabelled data, which means the input data is not associated with any known output value.

The purpose of the algorithm is to identify patterns and relationships in the data without any prior knowledge of what the data represents. Unsupervised learning algorithms can be used for tasks such as clustering, anomaly detection, and dimensionality reduction.

- **Reinforcement learning:** In reinforcement learning, the algorithm learns to make decisions by interacting with an environment and receiving feedback in the form of rewards or punishments. The goal of the algorithm is to learn a policy that maximizes the cumulative reward over time. Reinforcement learning algorithms can be used for tasks such as gaming, robotics, and autonomous vehicles.

Labelled data is data that has been manually annotated or labelled with known output values or target variables. In other words, labelled data is data that has been assigned a specific category or classification by a human expert. This means that the input data is already associated with known output values or target variables, making it ideal for use in supervised learning algorithms.

On the other hand, unlabelled data is data that has no known output values or target variables. In other words, the input data has not been manually annotated or categorised, and the algorithm must identify patterns and relationships in the data without any prior knowledge of what the data represents. This makes unlabelled data ideal for use in unsupervised learning algorithms.

And Finally, The Machine Learning Techniques

Machine learning is a large and complex field with many techniques and algorithms designed to solve a wide range of problems. Here are some of the most common techniques used in machine learning:

- **Regression:** Regression is a technique used to predict a continuous output variable based on one or more input variables. Linear regression is one of the most commonly used types of regression in machine learning, where the output variable is predicted using a linear function of the input variables.

- **Classification:** Classification is a technique used to predict a discrete output variable based on one or more input variables. This technique is commonly used in tasks such as image classification and spam filtering. Common classification algorithms include logistic regression, decision trees, and support vector machines.

- **Clustering:** Clustering is a technique used to group similar data points based on their characteristics. This technique is commonly used in tasks such as customer segmentation and image segmentation. Common clustering algorithms include k-means clustering, hierarchical clustering, and density-based clustering.

- **Dimensionality reduction:** Dimensionality reduction is a technique used to reduce the number of features or variables in a dataset without losing important information. This technique is commonly used in tasks such as data visualization and feature selection. Common dimensionality reduction algorithms include principal component analysis, t-SNE, and autoencoders.

- **Ensemble methods:** Ensemble methods are techniques that combine multiple machine learning models to improve their accuracy and robustness. This technique is commonly used in tasks such as predicting stock prices and detecting fraudulent transactions. Common ensemble methods include bagging, boosting, and random forests.

- **Deep learning:** Deep learning is a subset of machine learning that uses artificial neural networks to learn complex patterns and relationships in data. This technique is commonly used in tasks such as speech recognition, image classification and natural language processing. Common deep learning architectures include convolutional neural networks, recurrent neural networks, and transformers.

These are just a few of the many techniques used in machine learning. Each technique has its own strengths and weaknesses, and choosing the right technique for a particular task requires careful consideration of the data and the problem at hand. As machine learning continues to evolve, new techniques and algorithms will continue to be developed, making it an exciting and dynamic field.

Summary

In the first chapter of this book, we covered the basics of machine learning algorithms, including types of machine learning, labelled and unlabelled data, and techniques used in machine learning. We explored the three main types of machine learning algorithms, including supervised learning, unsupervised learning, and reinforcement learning, and discussed how labelled and unlabeled data is used in each. of these types. Additionally, we looked at six common machine learning techniques, including regression, classification, clustering, dimensionality reduction, ensemble methods, and deep learning. Each of these techniques is used to solve different types of problems and requires careful consideration of the data and the problem to be solved. As we progress through this book, we'll explore each of these techniques in more detail and discuss their applications in real-world business problems.

Chapter 2: Getting Started with Regression Algorithms

Regression is a statistical technique used to estimate the relationship between one or more independent variables and a dependent variable. It is a supervised learning technique commonly used in machine learning to predict continuous outcomes. Regression analysis allows us to model the relationship between the independent variables and the dependent variable and use this model to make predictions about new data.

Regression algorithms are machine learning algorithms that use regression analysis to predict continuous outcomes. In this chapter, we'll explore the most common regression algorithms used in machine learning, including:

- Linear Regression: Linear regression is the simplest type of regression algorithm used in machine learning. It models the relationship between the independent variables and the dependent variable using a linear function.

- Logistic Regression: Logistic regression is a type of regression algorithm used for classification problems. It models the probability of a binary outcome based on the independent variables.

- Multiple Regression: Multiple regression is an extension of linear regression that allows us to model the relationship between multiple independent variables and a single dependent variable.

- Polynomial Regression: Polynomial regression is a type of regression algorithm that models the relationship between the independent variables and the dependent variable using a polynomial function.

- Ridge Regression: Ridge Regression is a type of regression algorithm used to solve the problem of multicollinearity in multiple regression. It adds a regularization term to the cost function to avoid overfitting.

- Lasso Regression: Lasso regression is another type of regression algorithm used to solve the problem of multicollinearity in multiple regression. It uses a different type of regularization term than Ridge Regression.

- Elastic Net Regression: Elastic Net Regression is a combination of Ridge Regression and Lasso Regression. It uses both types of regularization terms to solve the problem of multicollinearity.

Linear Regression

Introduction

The Linear Regression algorithm is used to analyze the relationship between two variables, namely the independent variable (x) and the dependent variable (y). It helps us understand how changes in the independent variable affect the dependent variable. By fitting a line to the data, the algorithm allows us to make predictions or draw conclusions based on this relationship.

It works by finding the best-fitting line that minimizes the differences between the observed data points and the predicted values on the line. It achieves this through a process called "ordinary least squares" (OLS). The algorithm calculates the optimal values for the intercept

($β_0$) and slope ($β_1$) of the line that minimizes the sum of squared errors between the predicted values and the actual data points.

The mathematical formula for simple linear regression is

$$y = β_0 + β_1 x$$

Here, y represents the dependent variable, x represents the independent variable, $β_0$ represents the y-intercept (the value of y when x is zero), and $β_1$ represents the slope of the regression line (the change in y for a one-unit change in x).

Linear regression can be used in a variety of real-world business problems, such as predicting sales based on advertising spend, predicting the price of a house based on its features, or predicting the number of customer service calls depending on the time of day.

> **How to Identify if your problem can be solved using the Linear Regression algorithm?**
>
> To determine if a problem can be solved using linear regression, we need to determine if there is a linear relationship between the independent variables and the dependent variable. This can be done by plotting the data and looking for a linear pattern. We can also use correlation analysis to measure the strength of the relationship between variables. If the relationship is linear, linear regression may be a good candidate algorithm to use.

Implementation of Linear Regression

In this section, we will explore the implementation of the linear regression algorithm using Python. To implement linear regression and all other Machine Learning algorithms covered in this book, we will use the scikit-learn library.

> Scikit-learn is a popular Machine Learning library for Python that provides a range of tools for data mining and data analysis. It is built on top of NumPy, SciPy, and matplotlib, which are other popular Python libraries for scientific computing and data visualization.

To install scikit-learn, you can use pip, the package installer for Python. Open a terminal or command prompt and type the following command:

```
pip install -U scikit-learn
```

This will download and install the latest version of scikit-learn.

In addition to scikit-learn, we'll also need to install other libraries needed for this implementation, including NumPy, pandas, and Plotly. You can also install these libraries using pip:

```
pip install numpy pandas plotly
```

Now that we have the necessary libraries installed, let's implement linear regression using scikit-learn. We'll start by importing the necessary libraries:

```python
import numpy as np
import plotly.express as px
import plotly.graph_objects as go
from sklearn.model_selection import train_test_split
from sklearn.linear_model import LinearRegression
```

Let's create a complex dataset with a quadratic relationship between the independent variable x and the dependent variable y:

```python
# Step 1: Creating a complex dataset
```

```python
np.random.seed(0)
x = np.linspace(0, 10, 100) # Independent variable
y = 3 * x ** 2 + 2 * x + np.random.normal(0, 10, 100)
```

Now let's divide the data into training and test sets:

```python
# Step 2: Splitting the data into training and testing sets
x_train, x_test, y_train, y_test = train_test_split(x, y, test_size=0.2, random_state=42)
```

Now let's create an instance of LinearRegression class, and fit it to the training data:

```python
# Step 3: Implementing Linear Regression
model = LinearRegression()
x_train = x_train.reshape(-1, 1) # Reshaping x_train to a 2D array
model.fit(x_train, y_train) # Training the model
```

We have fitted the model to the training data and now we can use it to make predictions on the test data:

```python
x_test = x_test.reshape(-1, 1)
y_pred = model.predict(x_test)
```

Finally, we can visualize the results using the plotly library:

```python
# Step 5: Visualizing the results using Plotly
fig = go.Figure()
fig.add_trace(go.Scatter(x=x_test.flatten(), y=y_test, mode='markers', name='Actual Data'))

fig.add_trace(go.Scatter(x=x_test.flatten(), y=y_pred, mode='lines', name='Linear Regression Line'))

fig.update_layout(title='Linear Regression',
xaxis_title='Independent Variable (x)',
yaxis_title='Dependent Variable (y)')
fig.show()
```

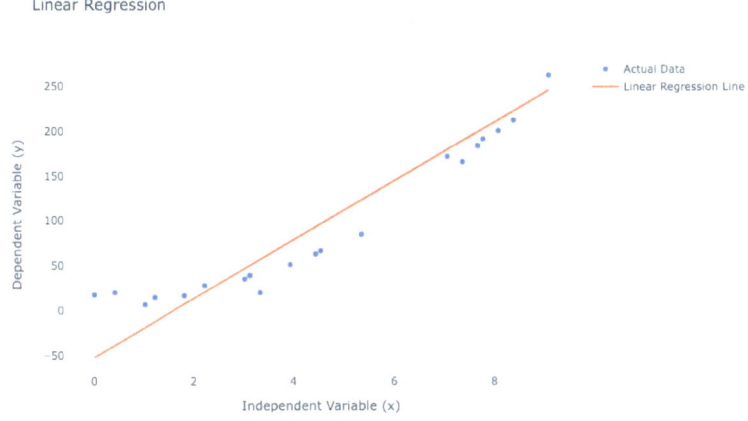

The slope of the line represents the relationship between the two variables. As you can see, the slope is positive, which means that as the independent variable increases, the dependent variable also increases.

Advantages & Disadvantages of Linear Regression

Linear regression has several advantages that make it a widely used algorithm. First, it is a simple and easy-to-understand algorithm that is well-suited for beginners in machine learning. Second, it is a parametric algorithm, which means it can be easily interpreted and explained. Third, it is highly scalable and can handle large data sets. However, the use of linear regression also has some disadvantages. For example, it assumes a linear relationship between independent and dependent variables, which is not always the case in real-world scenarios. Moreover, it is sensitive to outliers, which means that the presence of even a few extreme values can have a significant impact on the results. Finally, it may not work well when there are nonlinear relationships between variables.

Multiple Regression

Introduction

Multiple regression is a type of linear regression that allows more than one independent variable to be included in the model. The algorithm works by finding the line or plane of best fit that minimizes the sum of the squared errors between the predicted values and the actual values.

Multiple regression can be used in a variety of real-world business problems, such as predicting the price of a house based on location, size, and other characteristics, or estimating a company's revenue based on its advertising spend, number of employees, and other factors. It can also be used to identify the most significant factors contributing to the dependent variable and to quantify the strength and direction of their relationship.

> **How to Identify if your problem can be solved using Multiple Regression?**
>
> Determining whether a problem can be solved using multiple regression begins by looking at the relationships between the dependent variable and each independent variable. If there is a linear relationship between the dependent variable and two or more independent variables, multiple regression may be an appropriate approach. Additionally, it should be determined whether any confounding variables may affect the relationship between the independent and dependent variables. If so, these

> variables may need to be included in the model or controlled for in the analysis.

To implement a multiple regression model, you can implement the same steps on a dataset with multiple independent variables that you use to implement a simple regression model. If your data has multiple independent variables, the resulting model will be a multiple regression model rather than a simple regression model.

Polynomial Regression

Introduction

Polynomial Regression is a statistical algorithm used to model the relationship between a dependent variable and one or more independent variables. It is a type of regression analysis where the relationship between the variables is modelled as an nth-degree polynomial.

The Polynomial Regression algorithm works by fitting a polynomial equation to the data points, aiming to find the best-fitting curve that represents the relationship between the variables. It extends the linear regression model by introducing higher-degree polynomial terms, allowing for more flexible and curved relationships to be captured.

The mathematical formula for polynomial regression is:

$$y = \beta_0 + \beta_1 x + \beta_2 x^2 + \beta_3 x^3 + \ldots + \beta_n x^n + \varepsilon$$

Here, y represents the dependent variable, x represents the independent variable, and ε is the error term. The coefficients β_0, β_1, β_2,

... are the parameters that need to be estimated to determine the best-fitting polynomial curve.

> **How to Identify if your problem can be solved using Polynomial Regression?**
>
> To determine if a problem can be solved using polynomial regression, one must first examine the relationship between the independent and dependent variables. If there is a nonlinear relationship, such as a quadratic or cubic relationship, polynomial regression may be an appropriate approach.

Examples of Quadratic and Cubic relationships:

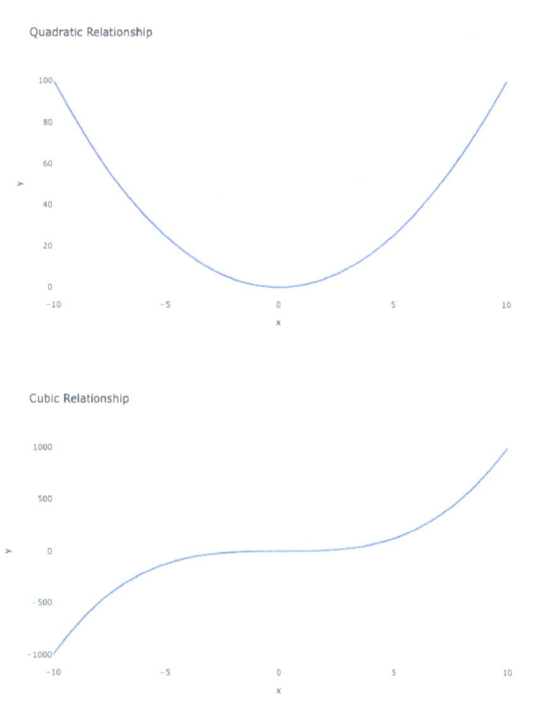

Implementation of Polynomial Regression

Now let's see how to implement the Polynomial Regression algorithm using Python. I'll start by importing the necessary Python libraries and creating the independent variable 'x' and the dependent variable 'y':

```python
import numpy as np
import matplotlib.pyplot as plt
from sklearn.preprocessing import PolynomialFeatures
from sklearn.linear_model import LinearRegression

np.random.seed(0)
x = np.linspace(0, 10, 100) # Independent variable
y = 3 * x ** 2 + 2 * x + np.random.normal(0, 10, 100) # Dependent variable with noise
```

Reshape the 'x' and 'y' arrays to column vectors:

```python
x = x.reshape(-1, 1)
y = y.reshape(-1, 1)
```

Split the data into training and testing sets:

```python
x_train, x_test, y_train, y_test = train_test_split(x, y, test_size=0.2, random_state=42)
```

Transform the independent variable 'x' into polynomial features:

```python
poly_features = PolynomialFeatures(degree=2)
x_train_poly = poly_features.fit_transform(x_train)
x_test_poly = poly_features.transform(x_test)
```

In the code above, we have created a polynomial feature object with a degree of 2. This will generate second-degree polynomial features. Next, we need to create an instance of the LinearRegression class and fit the polynomial characteristics to the model:

```python
model = LinearRegression()
model.fit(x_train_poly, y_train)
```

Generate predictions on training and test sets:

```python
y_train_pred = model.predict(x_train_poly)
y_test_pred = model.predict(x_test_poly)
```

Visualize the original data and the polynomial regression curve:

```python
import plotly.graph_objects as go

# Scatter plot for training data
trace_train = go.Scatter(x=x_train.flatten(), y=y_train.flatten(),
mode='markers', name='Training Data', marker=dict(color='blue'))

# Scatter plot for testing data
trace_test = go.Scatter(x=x_test.flatten(), y=y_test.flatten(),
mode='markers', name='Testing Data', marker=dict(color='green'))

# Line plot for polynomial regression
trace_regression = go.Scatter(x=x_train.flatten(), y=y_train_pred.flatten(),
mode='lines', name='Polynomial Regression', line=dict(color='red', width=2))

# Create the layout for the plot
layout = go.Layout(title='Polynomial Regression', xaxis=dict(title='x'),
yaxis=dict(title='y'))

# Combine the traces and layout and create the figure
figure = go.Figure(data=[trace_train, trace_test, trace_regression], layout=layout)

# Show the plot
figure.show()
```

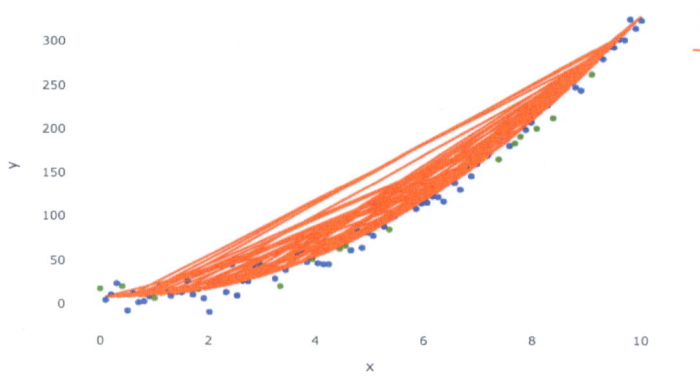

Advantages & Disadvantages of Polynomial Regression

The advantages of polynomial regression are that it can model nonlinear relationships between independent and dependent variables and can provide a better fit for the data than linear regression. However, the drawbacks are that it can be prone to overfitting if the degree of the polynomial is too high, and it can be computationally expensive for large data sets or high-degree polynomials.

Ridge Regression

Introduction

Ridge Regression is a statistical algorithm used in machine learning to handle the problem of multicollinearity, which occurs when predictor variables are highly correlated. It is an extension of the ordinary least squares regression method and is specifically designed to address the issue of overfitting in models with many variables.

Multicollinearity refers to the situation where predictor variables are highly correlated with each other. It can cause issues in traditional linear regression, such as unstable and unreliable coefficient estimates. However, Ridge Regression helps mitigate this problem by reducing the impact of multicollinearity.

The mathematical formula for ridge regression is:

$$\beta = (X^T X + \lambda I)^{-1} X^T y$$

where β is the vector of coefficients, X is the matrix of independent variables, y is the vector of values of dependent variables, λ is the penalty parameter, and I is the identity matrix.

Ridge Regression works by introducing a penalty term, controlled by the regularization parameter λ, to the ordinary least squares equation. This penalty term restricts the magnitude of the coefficient estimates, thereby reducing their sensitivity to small changes in the input data. By adding this penalty, Ridge Regression shrinks the coefficients towards zero, but they do not become exactly zero. This allows the algorithm to handle multicollinearity and provide more stable and reliable predictions.

> **How to Identify if your problem can be solved using Ridge Regression?**
>
> To determine if a problem can be solved using ridge regression, one must first determine if the independent variables are strongly correlated. This can be done by calculating the correlation matrix between the independent variables. If there is a strong correlation between the variables, ridge regression may be an appropriate algorithm. Additionally, if traditional regression models are overfitting or the model coefficients are large, ridge regression can be used to improve model accuracy.

Implementation of Ridge Regression

Now let's see how to implement the Ridge Regression algorithm using Python. We'll start by importing the necessary Python libraries and the dataset:

```python
import pandas as pd
from sklearn.datasets import load_diabetes
```

```python
data = load_diabetes()
X = pd.DataFrame(data.data, columns=data.feature_names)
y = pd.DataFrame(data.target, columns=["target"])
```

Next, we need to split the data into training and test sets:

```python
from sklearn.model_selection import train_test_split
X_train, X_test, y_train, y_test = train_test_split(X, y, test_size=0.2, random_state=0)
```

Next, we need to create an instance of the Ridge class and fit the model to the training data:

```python
from sklearn.linear_model import Ridge
regressor = Ridge(alpha=1.0)
regressor.fit(X_train, y_train)
```

In the code above, we've created an instance of the Ridge class with an alpha value of 1.0. This alpha value represents the penalty parameter, which determines the strength of the penalty term in the regression equation.

We can now make predictions on the test data:

```python
y_pred = regressor.predict(X_test)
```

To visualize the results, we can use the plotly library to create a scatter plot of the actual and predicted values:

```python
import plotly.graph_objs as go

fig = go.Figure()
fig.add_trace(go.Scatter(x=y_test["target"], y=y_pred.flatten(), mode="markers"))
fig.add_trace(go.Scatter(x=[0, 350], y=[0, 350], mode="lines"))
fig.update_layout(title="Actual vs Predicted", xaxis_title="Actual", yaxis_title="Predicted")
fig.show()
```

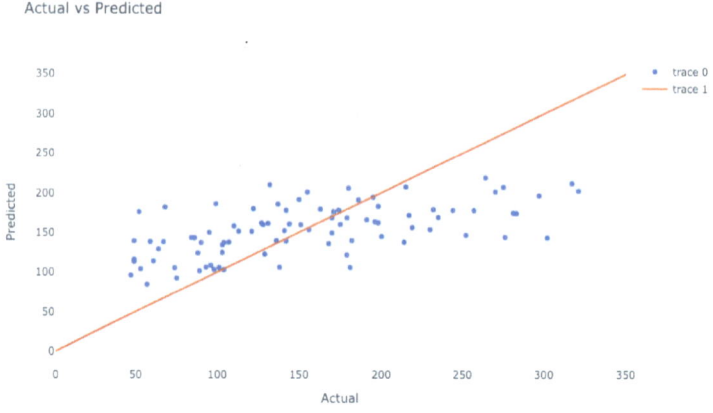

Advantages & Disadvantages of Ridge Regression

The main advantage of ridge regression is that it can handle highly correlated independent variables, avoid overfitting, and provide a better fit to the data than traditional linear regression. It does this by adding a penalty term to the regression equation, which limits the magnitude of the coefficients and helps prevent the model from adjusting for noise in the data.

The main disadvantage of ridge regression is that it can be difficult to determine the optimal value of the penalty parameter, and this value can vary depending on the data set being analyzed. Also, ridge regression assumes that the independent variables are normally distributed and linearly related to the dependent variable, which may not be true in all cases.

Lasso Regression

Introduction

Lasso regression is a type of regression algorithm used for feature selection and regularization. It is similar to ridge regression, but it adds an L1 penalty term to the regression equation, resulting in a sparse model where some of the coefficients are set to zero.

The mathematical formula for lasso regression is:

$$\beta = \operatorname{argmin}(\Sigma (y_i - \beta_0 - \Sigma_{j=1 \text{ to } p} x_{i,j}\beta_j)^2 + \lambda \Sigma |\beta_j|)$$

where β is the vector of coefficients, β0 is the intercept term, xi,j is the value of the jth independent variable for the ith observation, yi is the value of the dependent variable for the ith observation, λ is the parameter of penalty, and p is the number of independent variables.

In Lasso regression, the goal is to minimize the sum of squared residuals, just like in ordinary linear regression. However, Lasso introduces an additional term called the L1 penalty or the absolute value of the coefficients.

The L1 penalty encourages the coefficients of less important features to become exactly zero, effectively performing automatic feature selection. This characteristic sets Lasso regression apart from Ridge regression, where the coefficients are only shrunk towards zero but not exactly zero.

To achieve this, Lasso regression adjusts the coefficients during the model fitting process. As the penalty term increases, some coefficients are driven to zero, effectively excluding the corresponding features from the model.

The amount of shrinkage and feature selection in Lasso regression is controlled by a parameter called lambda or alpha. A higher value of lambda results in a more aggressive coefficient shrinking and a greater number of coefficients becoming zero.

Lasso regression is commonly used in real business problems where there are many independent variables, but only a few of them are important in predicting the dependent variable. This can happen in areas like finance or marketing, where many factors can affect results, but only a few are truly significant.

> **How to Identify if your problem can be solved using Lasso Regression?**
>
> To determine if a problem can be solved using lasso regression, one must first determine if there are many independent variables, but only a few are actually important in predicting the dependent variable. This can be done by performing an exploratory analysis of the data and examining the correlation matrix and scatter plots between the independent and dependent variables. If there are only a few significant correlations, lasso regression may be an appropriate algorithm to use. Additionally, if feature selection is required, lasso regression can be used to identify the independent variables that are most important in predicting the dependent variable.

Implementation of Lasso Regression

Now let's see how to implement the Lasso Regression algorithm using Python. We'll start by importing the necessary Python libraries and the dataset:

```
from sklearn.datasets import load_diabetes
```

```python
from sklearn.linear_model import Lasso
from sklearn.model_selection import train_test_split
import pandas as pd

data = load_diabetes()
X = pd.DataFrame(data.data, columns=data.feature_names)
y = pd.DataFrame(data.target, columns=["target"])
```

Next, we need to split the data into training and test sets:

```python
X_train, X_test, y_train, y_test = train_test_split(X, y, test_size=0.2, random_state=0)
```

Next, we need to create an instance of the Lasso class and fit the model to the training data:

```python
regressor = Lasso(alpha=1.0)
regressor.fit(X_train, y_train)
```

In the code above, we've created an instance of the Lasso class with an alpha value of 1.0. This alpha value represents the penalty parameter, which determines the strength of the penalty term in the regression equation.

We can now make predictions on the test data:

```python
y_pred = regressor.predict(X_test)
```

To visualize the results, we can use the plotly library to create a scatter plot of the actual and predicted values:

```python
import plotly.graph_objs as go

fig = go.Figure()
fig.add_trace(go.Scatter(x=y_test["target"], y=y_pred.flatten(), mode="markers"))
fig.add_trace(go.Scatter(x=[0, 350], y=[0, 350], mode="lines"))
fig.update_layout(title="Actual vs Predicted", xaxis_title="Actual", yaxis_title="Predicted")

fig.show()
```

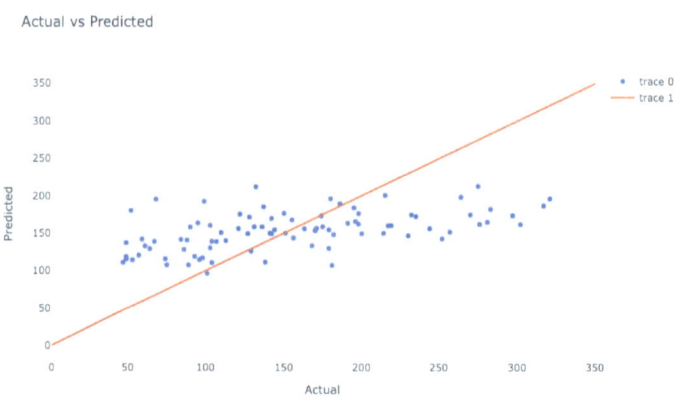

Advantages & Disadvantages of Lasso Regression

The main advantage of lasso regression is that it can handle highly correlated independent variables, prevent overfitting, and provide a sparse model with only the most important variables included. This is especially useful in situations where there are many independent variables, but only a few of them are important in predicting the dependent variable. Additionally, lasso regression provides a better fit to the data than traditional linear regression because it adds an L1 penalty term to the regression equation, resulting in a sparse model where some of the coefficients are set to zero.

The main disadvantage of lasso regression is that it can be difficult to determine the optimal value of the penalty parameter, and this value can vary depending on the data set being analyzed. Also, lasso regression assumes that the independent variables are normally distributed and linearly related to the dependent variable, which may not be true in all cases.

Elastic Net Regression

Introduction

Elastic net regression is a type of regression algorithm that combines the L1 and L2 penalties of Lasso and Ridge regression, respectively. It is used for feature selection and regularization and is particularly useful in situations where there are many independent variables and strongly correlated features.

The mathematical formula for elastic net regression is:

$$\beta = \operatorname{argmin}(\Sigma(y_i - \beta_0 - \Sigma_{j=1}^{p} x_{i,j}\beta_j)^2 + \lambda_1 \Sigma |\beta_j| + \lambda_2 \Sigma \beta_j^2)$$

where β is the vector of coefficients, β_0 is the term at the origin, $x_{i,j}$ is the value of the jth independent variable for the ith observation, y_i is the value of the dependent variable for the ith observation, λ_1 and λ_2 are the penalty parameters for the L1 and L2 penalties, respectively, and p is the number of independent variables.

Elastic net regression is commonly used in real business problems where there are many independent variables and highly correlated characteristics. For example, in finance, elastic net regression can be used to predict stock prices based on a large number of economic indicators, such as interest rates, inflation rates, and growth rates of GDP.

> **How to Identify if your problem can be solved using Elastic Net Regression?**
>
> To determine if a problem can be solved using elastic net regression, one must first determine if there are many independent

> variables and highly correlated characteristics in the data. This can be done by performing an exploratory analysis of the data and examining the correlation matrix and scatter plots between the independent and dependent variables. If there are many highly correlated features, elastic net regression may be an appropriate algorithm to use. Additionally, if it is necessary to select and regularize features, elastic net regression can be used to identify the independent variables that are most important in predicting the dependent variable.

Implementation of Elastic Net Regression

Now let's see how to implement the Elastic Net Regression algorithm using Python. We'll start by importing the necessary Python libraries and the dataset:

```
from sklearn.datasets import load_diabetes
from sklearn.linear_model import ElasticNet
from sklearn.model_selection import train_test_split
import pandas as pd

data = load_diabetes()
X = pd.DataFrame(data.data, columns=data.feature_names)
y = pd.DataFrame(data.target, columns=["target"])
```

Divide the dataset into training and test sets:

```
X_train, X_test, y_train, y_test = train_test_split(X, y, test_size=0.3, random_state=0)
```

Initialize the ElasticNet regression model with the desired parameters:

```
elastic_net = ElasticNet(alpha=0.5, l1_ratio=0.5, max_iter=10000, random_state=0)
```

Here, alpha is the penalty parameter that controls the strength of the regularization, l1_ratio is the blend parameter that controls the balance between L1 and L2 penalties, max_iter is the maximum number of iterations, and random_state is the seed used by the random number generator.

Finally, fit the model to the training data:

```
elastic_net.fit(X_train, y_train)
```

Advantages & Disadvantages of Elastic Net Regression

Elastic net regression has several advantages, including the ability to handle a large number of highly correlated predictors and features, and the ability to perform feature selection and regularization simultaneously. In addition, elastic net regression is less sensitive to outliers compared to other regression algorithms, which makes it more robust in the presence of noisy data.

However, elastic net regression also has some disadvantages, such as difficulty in choosing the optimal values for the penalty parameters, which can affect the performance of the model. Also, elastic net regression may not be suitable for datasets with a small number of observations or a large number of independent variables, as it may lead to overfitting. Overall, elastic net regression is a powerful tool for dealing with complex data sets and can provide accurate predictions when used appropriately.

Summary

The second chapter of this book looks at regression algorithms, which are used to model the relationship between a dependent variable and one or more independent variables. The chapter covers popular regression algorithms: linear regression, polynomial regression, ridge regression, lasso regression, and elastic net regression. For each algorithm, the chapter provides a detailed introduction, including an explanation of how the algorithm works, the mathematical formula underlying the algorithm, an example of a real business problem where the algorithm can be used, and how to identify if the problem can be solved using the algorithm. The chapter also includes step-by-step explanations and Python implementations of each algorithm using appropriate datasets. The advantages and disadvantages of each algorithm are also discussed in detail, along with the meaning of the parameters used in each algorithm. Overall, this chapter provides a comprehensive overview of regression algorithms and their applications, providing readers with the knowledge needed to effectively use these algorithms in real-world scenarios.

Chapter 3: Linear Classification Algorithms

Classification is a fundamental task in machine learning, in which we aim to predict a discrete class label for a given input. Linear classification algorithms are a type of machine learning algorithm that uses a linear decision boundary to separate different classes of data.

Logistic regression is one such linear classification algorithm which, despite its name, is used for classification rather than regression. In logistic regression, the algorithm estimates the probability that the input belongs to each class and then assigns the input to the class with the highest probability. This probability estimate is obtained by applying the logistic function (also known as the sigmoid function) to a linear combination of the input features.

In addition to logistic regression, we will cover several other linear classification algorithms in this chapter. These include:

- Linear Discriminant Analysis (LDA): LDA is a generative model that assumes the input features are normally distributed and estimates the mean and covariance of the features for each class. LDA then uses these estimates to calculate the posterior probability of each class and assigns the entry to the class with the highest probability.

- Stochastic Gradient Descent (SGD) Classifier: The SGD classifier is a variant of linear regression in which we use stochastic gradient descent to optimize the linear function for classification purposes.

Now let's explore these algorithms in detail.

Logistic Regression

Introduction

Logistic regression is a popular algorithm used to solve classification problems in machine learning. Unlike linear regression, which predicts a continuous output variable, logistic regression is used to predict the probability of an event occurring. The algorithm works by modelling the relationship between a set of independent variables and a binary dependent variable, which can take one of two possible outcomes, such as "yes" or "no".

The mathematical formula behind logistic regression is based on the logistic function, which takes the form of an S-shaped curve. The logistic function is used to transform the linear regression equation into a probability value between 0 and 1, which can then be used to perform binary classifications. The formula for logistic regression is:

$$p = 1 / (1 + e\wedge\text{-}(b0 + b1x1 + b2x2 + \ldots + bnxn))$$

where p is the predicted probability of the event occurring, e is the base of the natural logarithm, b0 is the intercept term, bx is the coefficient of the independent variable x, and n is the number of independent variables.

Logistic regression can be used in many real-world business problems, such as predicting whether or not a customer will buy a product based on their demographic information, predicting whether or not a loan application will be approved based on the applicant's financial history, and predicting whether a patient has a disease or not based on their symptoms and medical history. If the problem involves predicting a binary outcome (yes/no, true/false, 0/1), logistic regression may be an appropriate algorithm.

> **How to Identify if your problem can be solved using the Logistic Regression algorithm?**
>
> To determine if the problem you are working on can be solved using logistic regression, you need to determine if the dependent variable is binary or categorical. If the dependent variable has only two possible outcomes, logistic regression can be used to predict the probability of each outcome. Also, logistic regression assumes that there is a linear relationship between the independent variables and the log probability of the dependent variable and that the residuals are normally distributed. If these assumptions are satisfied, logistic regression can be used to model the probability of the event occurring.

Implementation of Logistic Regression

Let's go through the implementation of logistic regression in Python step by step. First, we need to import the necessary libraries:

```python
import numpy as np
from sklearn.linear_model import LogisticRegression
from sklearn.datasets import load_breast_cancer
from sklearn.model_selection import train_test_split
```

Next, we load the breast cancer dataset, which is already available in scikit-learn.

```python
data = load_breast_cancer()
X = data.data
y = data.target
```

We divide the dataset into training and testing sets:

```
X_train, X_test, y_train, y_test = train_test_split(X, y, test_size=0.2,
random_state=42)
```

Next, we create an instance of the logistic regression model and fit it to the training data:

```
model = LogisticRegression()
model.fit(X_train, y_train)
```

Once the model is trained, we can use it to make predictions on the test data:

```
y_pred = model.predict(X_test)
print(y_pred)
```

We can also evaluate the performance of the model by calculating the accuracy score:

```
accuracy = model.score(X_test, y_test)
print("Accuracy:", accuracy)
```

Accuracy: 0.9649122807017544

Advantages & Disadvantages of Logistic Regression

The Logistic Regression algorithm has several advantages, including its simplicity and ease of implementation. It is also efficient and performs well on smaller datasets with a small feature set. Additionally, logistic regression provides interpretable results, making it easier to understand and communicate with stakeholders.

However, logistic regression also has some limitations. It cannot handle nonlinear relationships between independent and dependent variables, and it is prone to overfitting if there are too many features or the dataset is unbalanced.

Linear Discriminant Analysis (LDA)

Introduction

Linear discriminant analysis (LDA) is a linear classification algorithm commonly used to solve classification problems. LDA is a generative model that finds a linear combination of input features that best separates different classes.

The algorithm assumes that the input features are normally distributed and estimates the feature mean and covariance for each class. It then uses these estimates to calculate the posterior probability for each class and assigns the input to the class with the highest probability.

The mathematical formula of LDA is to find a linear discriminant function, which is a linear combination of the input features that maximizes the ratio of between-class variance to within-class variance. This function is given by:

$$w = (S_w^{-1} * (m_1 - m_2))$$

where w is the discriminant vector, S_w^{-1} is the inverse of the intra-class covariance matrix, m1 and m2 are the mean vectors of the two classes, and * represents the matrix multiplication.

LDA can be used in a variety of real-world business problems, such as predicting whether or not a customer will buy a product based on their demographic information. Another example is medical diagnostics, where LDA can be used to distinguish healthy from diseased individuals based on their clinical parameters.

> **How to Identify if your problem can be solved using Linear Discriminant Analysis?**
>
> To determine if LDA is suitable for a given problem, we need to ensure that the input features are normally distributed and the classes are separable. LDA works best when the number of features in the data is low.

Implementation of LDA

Let's go through the implementation of LDA in Python step by step. For this purpose, we can use the Breast Cancer Wisconsin (Diagnosis) dataset, which is also available in the scikit-learn library. This dataset is based on a binary classification problem, where the goal is to classify breast cancer tumours as malignant or benign based on various characteristics:

```
from sklearn.datasets import load_breast_cancer
from sklearn.discriminant_analysis import LinearDiscriminantAnalysis
breast_cancer = load_breast_cancer()
X = breast_cancer.data
y = breast_cancer.target
```

Now initialize the LDA model:

```
lda = LinearDiscriminantAnalysis()
lda.fit(X, y)
```

Now we transform the data using the LDA model:

```
X_lda = lda.transform(X)
```

In the code above, X and y represent the input characteristics and target variables of the Wisconsin Breast Cancer (Diagnosis) dataset, respectively. We then initialize the LDA model using LinearDiscriminantAnalysis() and fit it to the dataset using fit(X, y).

Finally, we transform the dataset using the LDA model using the transform(X) method.

Once we have transformed the dataset, we can use it for classification tasks:

```
from sklearn.model_selection import train_test_split

X_train, X_test, y_train, y_test = train_test_split(X_lda, y, test_size=0.2, random_state=42)

from sklearn.linear_model import LogisticRegression

classifier = LogisticRegression()
classifier.fit(X_train, y_train)
```

Advantages & Disadvantages of LDA

Linear discriminant analysis (LDA) has several advantages, such as its simplicity, efficiency in high-dimensional data, and ability to handle small sample sizes. LDA can also reduce data dimensionality while preserving class separability, which can improve the performance of classification algorithms.

However, LDA assumes that the data is normally distributed and the class covariances are equal, which may not be true in some real-world scenarios. LDA may also suffer from overfitting if the number of samples is small compared to the number of features, and it may not be suitable for nonlinearly separable data. Overall, LDA is a useful linear classification algorithm that can be efficient in many practical applications, but its limitations should also be considered.

Stochastic Gradient Descent Classifier

Introduction

The stochastic gradient descent (SGD) classifier is a linear classification algorithm that uses an iterative optimization technique to minimize the error between the predicted class labels and the true class labels. The algorithm works by updating model parameters (weights) using a small subset of the training data on each iteration, making it particularly suitable for large datasets.

The mathematical formula behind the SGD classification algorithm is:

$$y = f(w^T * x)$$

where y is the predicted output (0 or 1), x is the input features, w is the weight vector, and f is the activation function (usually the logistic function or the softmax function). During training, the algorithm updates the weights using the following rule:

$$w\_new = w\_old - \eta * \nabla(loss)$$

where w_new and w_old are the updated and previous weight vectors, η is the learning rate, and ∇(loss) is the gradient of the loss function with respect to the weights. The loss function measures the difference between the predicted class labels and the true class labels, and the gradient tells the algorithm how to adjust the weights to minimize the error.

The stochastic gradient descent classifier can be used in many real-world business problems, such as sentiment analysis of customer reviews, spam detection in emails, or fraud detection in financial transactions. The algorithm can efficiently handle large data sets and can also be used in e-learning scenarios where new data is continuously coming in.

> **How to Identify if your problem can be solved using SGD Classifier?**
>
> To determine if the problem can be solved using the SGD Classifier, we need to check if the data is linearly separable and the number of features is large. If the classes can be separated by a linear decision boundary and the number of features is large, SGD Classifier can be used to classify the data. However, if the data is not linearly separable or the number of features is small, other linear or nonlinear classification algorithms may be more appropriate.

Implementation of SGD Classification Algorithm

Let's go through the implementation of the SGD Classifier in Python step by step. We'll start by importing the necessary Python libraries and creating a sample dataset:

```python
from sklearn.datasets import make_classification
from sklearn.model_selection import train_test_split
from sklearn.linear_model import SGDClassifier

# Generate a binary classification dataset
X, y = make_classification(n_samples=1000, n_features=10, n_classes=2, random_state=42)

# Split the data into training and testing sets
X_train, X_test, y_train, y_test = train_test_split(X, y, test_size=0.2, random_state=42)
```

Now create an instance of SGDClassifier and set the hyperparameters:

```python
clf = SGDClassifier(loss='log', penalty='l2', alpha=0.0001, max_iter=1000, tol=1e-3, random_state=42)
```

Here we set the loss function to "log" for binary classification, the penalty to "l2" for ridge regularization, the learning rate to 0.0001, the maximum number of iterations to 1000, the tolerance on 1e-3 and the random seed at 42.

Now train the model on the training data:

```
clf.fit(X_train, y_train)
```

Advantages & Disadvantages of SGD Classification Algorithm

On the positive side, the SGD classifier is efficient, fast, and scalable, which makes it well-suited for large datasets. Moreover, it can handle both linear and nonlinear models and be used for binary and multi-class classification problems.

However, it can be sensitive to the choice of hyperparameters and prone to overfitting if not tuned correctly. Moreover, the SGD classifier may not always converge to the global optimum, which leads to suboptimal results. Therefore, proper parameter tuning and careful selection of features are essential to achieve optimal performance with the SGD classifier.

Summary

The chapter began with an introduction to classification and linear classification algorithms, emphasizing the importance of these algorithms for separating different classes of data. Logistic regression, linear discriminant analysis (LDA), and stochastic gradient descent (SGD) classifier have been discussed as key linear classification algorithms. Each algorithm has been explained in detail, including how it works, the mathematical formulas behind it, and the real business problems they can be applied. The chapter also provided information on identifying when a problem can be solved using each algorithm. Additionally, Python implementations have been provided, showing the practical application of the algorithms using appropriate datasets. Finally, the advantages and disadvantages of each algorithm have been summarized, allowing readers to understand the strengths and limitations of these linear classification techniques. Overall, this chapter has provided a comprehensive understanding of linear classification algorithms and their importance in solving classification problems.

Chapter 4: Performance Evaluation Methods

In the field of machine learning, accurate performance evaluation of models is essential to understand the performance of our models and make informed decisions. This chapter dives into the world of performance evaluation methods, explaining why they are essential in the machine learning workflow. So far we have covered linear regression and linear classification algorithms. Now, before diving into the other complex machine learning algorithms, it is crucial to cover a full range of evaluation metrics based on regression and classification tasks.

Performance evaluation methods allow us to quantify the effectiveness and efficiency of our models by providing measurable measures that reflect their predictive capabilities. By evaluating the models, we get information about their strengths, weaknesses and overall performance, which allows us to compare different models and make informed decisions.

To ensure a comprehensive understanding of model evaluation, this chapter will cover a wide range of regression and classification evaluation measures. These measures allow us to evaluate the performance of our models in terms of accuracy, precision, recall, F1 score, root mean square error and many others. By digging deeper into these metrics, readers will be equipped with the knowledge to evaluate the model's performance in a variety of tasks.

Classification Performance Evaluation Metrics

Introduction

Classification tasks involve predicting categorical labels for input data, and having robust evaluation metrics that capture the nuances of these predictions is crucial. These metrics allow us to assess the quality of our models by assessing their predictive abilities in different classes and quantifying their performance in terms of accuracy, precision, recall, F1 score, etc.

Accuracy, one of the fundamental measures, measures the proportion of correctly classified instances. **Precision** measures the proportion of true positive predictions out of all positive predictions, with an emphasis on the ability to minimize false positives. **Recall**, on the other hand, measures the proportion of true positive predictions and overall true positive instances, focusing on minimizing false negatives. The **F1 score** combines precision and recall, providing a balanced measure of a model's performance. The **confusion matrix** displays the number of true positive, true negative, false positive, and false negative predictions.

Additionally, this chapter will explore other valuable classification parameters such as the area under the receiver operating characteristics **(ROC)** curve, which captures the trade-off between true positive rate and false positive rate, and the confusion matrix, which provides a comprehensive overview of model performance in different classes.

Accuracy

Accuracy is a crucial evaluation metric that provides insight into the performance of classification models. It measures the overall accuracy of predictions made by a model, revealing how well it ranks instances. Accuracy is determined by comparing the number of correctly classified instances to the total number of instances in the dataset.

The mathematical formula behind precision is simple yet powerful. It is calculated by dividing the number of correct predictions by the total number of instances:

Accuracy = (Number of correct predictions) / (Total number of instances)

The desired result for accuracy is a high score because it indicates a model that made a large number of correct predictions. A high accuracy score implies that the model performs well in classifying instances and capturing underlying patterns in the data.

Let's train a Machine Learning model to evaluate it using accuracy and all other classification evaluation metrics:

```python
from sklearn.datasets import make_classification
from sklearn.model_selection import train_test_split
from sklearn.linear_model import SGDClassifier

# Generate a binary classification dataset
X, y = make_classification(n_samples=1000, n_features=10, n_classes=2, random_state=42)

# Split the data into training and testing sets
X_train, X_test, y_train, y_test = train_test_split(X, y, test_size=0.2, random_state=42)

clf = SGDClassifier(loss='log', penalty='l2', alpha=0.0001, max_iter=1000, tol=1e-3, random_state=42)

clf.fit(X_train, y_train)
y_pred = clf.predict(X_test)
```

Till now we have trained the model, now here's how to evaluate the model using accuracy:

```python
# Predict the class labels for the test set
y_pred = clf.predict(X_test)

# Evaluate the model's performance using accuracy
from sklearn.metrics import accuracy_score
accuracy = accuracy_score(y_test, y_pred)
```

```
print("Accuracy:", accuracy)
```

Accuracy: 0.835

An accuracy score of 0.835 suggests that the classification model achieved an overall accuracy rate of 83.5% on the test dataset. This indicates that the model correctly classified approximately 83.5% of the instances in the test set.

An accuracy score between 0 and 1 represents the proportion of correct predictions made by the model. In this case, the model has achieved reasonably good accuracy, indicating that it has learned patterns and relationships in the data and is making accurate predictions most of the time.

Precision

Precision is a crucial evaluation metric used to assess the performance of a classification model. It measures the proportion of true positive predictions and overall positive predictions made by the model. Precision provides information about the model's ability to accurately identify positive instances, with an emphasis on minimizing false positive predictions.

Mathematically, precision is calculated by dividing the number of true positive predictions by the sum of true positives and false positives:

Precision = true positives / (true positives + false positives)

The desired result for precision is a high score because it indicates that the model makes a minimal number of false positive predictions. In other words, the model correctly identifies positive instances without misclassifying negative instances as positive.

Precision is especially useful in scenarios where the cost of false positive predictions is high, such as in medical diagnostics or spam detection. In such cases, it is crucial to minimize false positive predictions to avoid unnecessary processing or incorrect reporting of legitimate emails as spam.

Here's how to use precision to evaluate the performance of your classification model:

```
from sklearn.metrics import precision_score
precision = precision_score(y_test, y_pred)
print("Precision: ", precision)

Precision:  0.8362068965517241
```

A precision score of 0.836 indicates that the classification model achieved an accuracy rate of 83.6% on the test dataset. Precision measures the proportion of true positive predictions out of all positive predictions made by the model.

A precision score between 0 and 1 represents the model's ability to accurately identify positive instances. In this case, the model achieved reasonably good precision, suggesting that it makes correct positive predictions about 83.6% of the time.

Recall

Recall, also known as sensitivity or true positive rate, is an important evaluation metric used to assess the performance of a classification model. It measures the proportion of true positive predictions out of all true positive instances in the data set.

Recall provides information about the model's ability to correctly identify positive instances, with an emphasis on minimizing false negative predictions. It aims to capture as many positive instances as possible, avoiding the scenario where actual positive instances are incorrectly classified as negative.

Mathematically, recall is calculated by dividing the number of true positive predictions by the sum of true positive predictions and false negative predictions:

Recall = true positives / (true positives + false negatives)

The desired outcome for recall is a high score, indicating that the model successfully captures a large proportion of positive instances. A high recall score suggests that the model effectively minimizes false negatives and correctly identifies positives.

Here's how to use recall to evaluate the performance of your classification model:

```
from sklearn.metrics import recall_score
recall = recall_score(y_test, y_pred)
print("Recall: ", recall)

Recall:  0.8738738738738738
```

A recall score of 0.87 indicates that the classification model achieved an 87% recall rate on the test dataset.

A recall score between 0 and 1 represents the model's ability to capture positive instances. In this case, the model achieved relatively high recall, suggesting that it correctly identifies about 87% of the positives in the dataset.

F1 Score

The F1 score is a widely used evaluation measure that combines precision and recall into a single measure, providing a balanced assessment of a classification model's performance. It quantifies the trade-off between precision and recall, providing insight into the model's ability to simultaneously minimize false positives and false negatives.

The F1 score is calculated using the harmonic mean of precision and recall, giving equal weight to both measures. Mathematically, it is defined by:

*F1 score = 2 * (Precision * Recall) / (Precision + Recall)*

The F1 score ranges from 0 to 1, with a higher score indicating better model performance. The desired result for the F1 score is a high value, suggesting that the model strikes a balance between precision and recall, effectively minimizing false positives and false negatives.

Here's how to use the F1 Score to evaluate the performance of your classification model:

```
from sklearn.metrics import f1_score
f1score = f1_score(y_test, y_pred)
print("F1 Score: ", f1score)
```

```
F1 Score:  0.8546255506607928
```

The F1 score ranges from 0 to 1, with a higher score indicating better model performance. In this case, an F1 score of 0.85 suggests that the model strikes a relatively good balance between precision and recall. This indicates that the model can make accurate positive predictions while minimizing the number of false positives and false negatives.

Confusion Matrix

Confusion matrix is a powerful tool used in classification tasks to provide a detailed and organized summary of the model's predictions and the actual class labels of instances in the dataset. It helps to evaluate the performance of a classification model by visually representing the number of correct and incorrect predictions.

The confusion matrix is structured as a table that includes four important components: true positives (TP), true negatives (TN), false positives (FP), and false negatives (FN). Each component represents the number or number of instances falling into a particular prediction category.

	Predicted Positive	Predicted Negative
Actual Positive	True Positives (TP)	False Negatives (FN)
Actual Negative	False Positives (FP)	True Negatives (TN)

The desired result for the confusion matrix is to have a high number of true positives and true negatives while minimizing the number of false positives and false negatives. A balanced and accurate model would ideally have high values for TP and TN, and low values for FP and FN.

Here's how to use confusion matrix to evaluate the performance of your classification model:

```
from sklearn.metrics import confusion_matrix
cm = confusion_matrix(y_test, y_pred)
print("Confusion Matrix:")
print(cm)
```

```
Confusion Matrix:
[[70 19]
 [14 97]]
```

Looking at the matrix:

- The top left cell represents the number of true positives (TP), which is 70. These are cases where the model correctly predicted the positive class.

- The top right cell represents the number of false negatives (FN), which is 19. These are cases where the model incorrectly predicted the negative class when the actual class was positive.
- The bottom left cell represents the number of false positives (FP), which is 14. These are cases where the model incorrectly predicted the positive class when the actual class was negative.
- The bottom right cell represents the number of true negatives (TN), which is 97. These are cases where the model correctly predicted the negative class.

AUC & ROC

The area under the curve (AUC) and receiver operating characteristics (ROC) curve are common evaluation measures used in binary classification tasks. They provide insight into the performance and discriminating power of a classification model.

The ROC curve is a graphical representation of the model's performance at different classification thresholds. It plots the true positive rate (TPR) against the false positive rate (FPR) for different threshold values. The TPR represents the proportion of true positive instances correctly classified as positive, while the FPR represents the proportion of true negative instances incorrectly classified as positive.

AUC is the numerical value that represents the area under the ROC curve. It summarizes the ability of the model to distinguish between positive and negative classes for all possible threshold values.

The image below shows an example of the desired AUC and ROC.

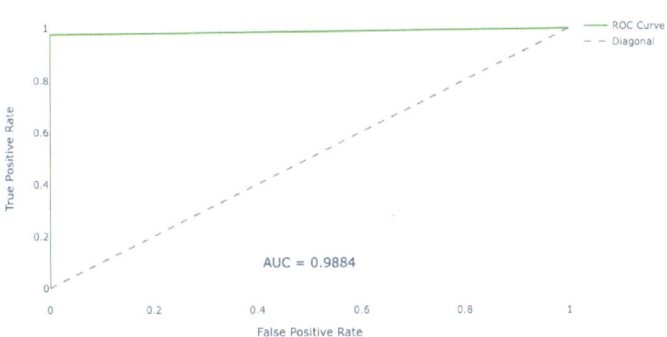

A higher AUC score indicates a better-performing model with a greater ability to discriminate between classes. The ROC curve, when closer to the upper left corner, demonstrates a higher true positive rate (TPR) versus false positive rate (FPR) across various classification thresholds. This indicates that the model has a better balance between correctly identifying positive instances and minimizing false positive errors.

Here's how to use AUC & ROC to evaluate the performance of your classification model:

```python
import plotly.graph_objects as go
from sklearn.metrics import roc_auc_score, roc_curve

# Calculating the false positive rate, true positive rate, and AUC
fpr, tpr, thresholds = roc_curve(y_test, y_pred)
auc = roc_auc_score(y_test, y_pred)

# Creating the ROC curve
roc_trace = go.Scatter(
    x=fpr,
    y=tpr,
    name="ROC Curve",
    mode="lines",
    line=dict(color="green")
)

# Creating the diagonal line
diag_trace = go.Scatter(
```

```python
    x=[0, 1],
    y=[0, 1],
    name="Diagonal",
    mode="lines",
    line=dict(color="gray", dash="dash")
)

# Creating the layout
layout = go.Layout(
    title="AUC & ROC Curve",
    xaxis=dict(title="False Positive Rate"),
    yaxis=dict(title="True Positive Rate"),
    showlegend=True,
)

# Creating the figure
fig = go.Figure(data=[roc_trace, diag_trace], layout=layout)

# Adding the AUC score to the plot
fig.add_annotation(
    x=0.5,
    y=0.1,
    text=f"AUC = {auc:.4f}",
    showarrow=False,
    font=dict(size=16),
)

# Show the plot
fig.show()
```

AUC & ROC Curve

AUC = 0.8302

An AUC score of 0.8302 implies that, on average, the model correctly ranks a randomly selected positive instance higher than a randomly selected negative instance about 83.02% of the time. This indicates that the model has a satisfactory level of discrimination between classes.

Regression Performance Evaluation Metrics

Introduction

Regression metrics are quantitative measures used to evaluate the performance of regression models. They provide information about how well a regression model fits the data and how accurately it predicts the outcome variable. These metrics allow us to assess the model's ability to capture underlying relationships and make reliable predictions.

In this section, we will explore a range of regression performance evaluation measures that provide valuable insight into model accuracy, reliability, and robustness. Here, we'll cover a variety of widely used regression evaluation metrics, including mean squared error (MSE), root mean squared error (RMSE), mean absolute error (MAE), R-squared (R^2) and the adjusted R-squared (R^2_adj).

Mean Squared Error

Mean squared error (MSE) is a widely used regression evaluation metric that measures the mean squared difference between the predicted and actual values of the target variable. It provides information about the overall accuracy and precision of the regression model.

MSE works by calculating the squared differences between each predicted value and its corresponding actual value. These differences are then averaged to obtain the MSE score. By squaring the differences, MSE emphasizes larger errors, making it sensitive to outliers.

Mathematically, the mean square error is calculated using the following formula:

$$MSE = (1/n) * \Sigma (y_i - \hat{y}_i)^2$$

where:

- n is the total number of data points,
- yi represents the actual value of the target variable,
- ŷi represents the predicted value of the target variable.

The desired result for the mean squared error is to get a lower value, indicating a regression model that closely aligns the predicted values with the actual values. A lower MSE suggests better accuracy and lower average prediction error.

Now let's train a regression model to show the implementation of MSE and all other regression metrics that we will cover in this chapter:

```python
from sklearn.datasets import load_diabetes
from sklearn.linear_model import LinearRegression
from sklearn.model_selection import train_test_split

# Load the diabetes dataset
diabetes_data = load_diabetes()

# Select features and target variable
X = diabetes_data.data
y = diabetes_data.target

# Split the data into training and testing sets
X_train, X_test, y_train, y_test = train_test_split(X, y, test_size=0.2, random_state=42)

# Train a linear regression model
```

```
model = LinearRegression()
model.fit(X_train, y_train)

# Make predictions on the test set
y_pred = model.predict(X_test)
```

Here's how to use MSE to evaluate the performance of a regression model:

```
# Compute the Mean Squared Error
from sklearn.metrics import mean_squared_error
mse = mean_squared_error(y_test, y_pred)
print("Mean Squared Error:", mse)
```

Mean Squared Error: 2900.193628493482

The MSE score quantifies the mean square difference between predicted and actual values in a regression model. In our case, an MSE score of 2900.19 suggests that, on average, the predictions made by the model differ from the actual values by about 2900.19 squared units.

A higher MSE value indicates that the model has a larger average prediction error. In other words, the model's predictions are less accurate and further from the actual values. In this case, an MSE of 2900.19 suggests that the regression model might not capture underlying patterns and relationships in the data as effectively as desired.

Root Mean Squared Error

Root mean square error (RMSE) is a widely used regression evaluation metric that measures the average magnitude of prediction errors in a regression model. It is a variant of the mean squared error (MSE) but provides the result in the original scale of the target variable.

RMSE works by calculating the square root of the root mean square difference between predicted and actual values. This captures the typical size of errors made by the model and provides a more interpretable measure.

Mathematically, the root mean square error is calculated using the following formula:

$$RMSE = sqrt((1/n) * \Sigma (y_i - ŷ_i)^2)$$

Where:

- n is the total number of data points,
- yi represents the actual value of the target variable,
- ŷi represents the predicted value of the target variable.

The desired result for the root mean square error is to get a lower value, indicating a regression model that has smaller prediction errors and is more accurate in its predictions. A lower RMSE suggests a better fit of the model to the data and more accurate predictions.

Here's how to use RMSE to evaluate the performance of a regression model:

```
from sklearn.metrics import mean_squared_error
import numpy as np

mse = mean_squared_error(y_test, y_pred)
rmse = np.sqrt(mse)
print("Root Mean Squared Error:", rmse)
```

Root Mean Squared Error: 53.85344583676593

An RMSE score of 53.85 indicates that, on average, model predictions deviate from actual values by approximately 53.85 units. This suggests the need for further refinement and evaluation of the model to obtain more accurate predictions and improve the overall performance of the regression model.

Mean Absolute Error

Mean Absolute Error (MAE) is a common regression evaluation metric that measures the mean absolute difference between predicted and actual values in a regression model. It provides a measure of the magnitude of prediction errors.

MAE works by calculating the average of the absolute differences between the predicted and actual values. This captures the typical size of errors made by the model and provides a more interpretable measure.

Mathematically, the mean absolute error is calculated using the following formula:

$$MAE = (1/n) * \Sigma |y_i - \hat{y}_i|$$

Where:

- n is the total number of data points,
- yi represents the actual value of the target variable,
- ŷi represents the predicted value of the target variable.

The desired result for the mean absolute error is to get a lower value, indicating a regression model that has smaller prediction errors and is more accurate in its predictions. A lower MAE suggests a better fit of the model to the data and more accurate predictions.

Here's how to use MAE to evaluate the performance of a regression model:

```python
from sklearn.metrics import mean_absolute_error

mae = mean_absolute_error(y_test, y_pred)
print("Mean Absolute Error:", mae)
```

Mean Absolute Error: 42.79409467959994

An MAE score of 42.79 indicates that, on average, the model's predictions deviate from the actual values by about 42.79 units. This suggests the need for further refinement and evaluation of the model to obtain more accurate predictions and improve the overall performance of the regression model.

R-squared

R-squared, also known as the coefficient of determination, is a widely used regression evaluation metric that measures the proportion of the variance of the dependent variable that can be explained by the independent variables in a regression model. It indicates the fit of the regression model to the data.

R-squared works by comparing the variation in predicted values to the variation in actual values. It quantifies the proportion of the total variation of the dependent variable that is accounted for by the regression model. The R-squared ranges from 0 to 1, with higher values indicating a better fit of the model to the data.

Mathematically, R-squared is calculated using the following formula:

R-squared = 1 - (Sum of squares of residuals / Total sum of squares)

Where:

- The sum of the squares of the residuals is the sum of the squared differences between the predicted and actual values.
- The total sum of squares is the sum of the squared differences between the actual values and their mean.

The desired result for the R-squared is to obtain a higher value, closer to 1. A higher R-squared indicates that a greater proportion of the variance of the dependent variable is explained by the independent variables in the model of regression. This suggests a better fit of the model to the data and more accurate predictions.

Here's how to use R-squared to evaluate the performance of a regression model:

```
from sklearn.metrics import r2_score
r2 = r2_score(y_test, y_pred)
print("R-squared:", r2)
```

R-squared: 0.4526027629719195

An R-squared score of 0.45 suggests that the regression model explains about 45% of the variation in the dependent variable. This indicates the need for further investigation and possibly refinement of the model to achieve a higher degree of explanation and improve its overall performance.

Adjusted R-squared

Adjusted R-squared is a variation of the R-squared metric that takes into account the number of independent variables used in a regression model. It provides an adjusted measure of the fit of the model to the data, taking into account the complexity of the model and the potential for overfitting.

Adjusted R-squared works by penalizing the inclusion of unnecessary variables in the model. It adjusts the R-squared value by incorporating the number of independent variables and the sample size, providing a more conservative assessment of the model's goodness of fit.

Mathematically, the adjusted R-squared is calculated using the following formula:

*Adjusted R-squared = 1 - [(1 - R-squared) * (n - 1) / (n - k - 1)]*

Where:

- R-squared is the standard R-squared value,
- n is the sample size, and
- k is the number of independent variables in the model.

The desired result for the adjusted R-squared is to obtain a higher value, closer to 1. A higher adjusted R-squared indicates that the model can explain a greater proportion of the variance of the dependent variable, even after taking into account the number of independent variables and potential overfitting.

Here's how to use the adjusted R-squared to evaluate the performance of a regression model:

```python
from sklearn.metrics import r2_score

r2 = r2_score(y_test, y_pred)
n = len(y_test)
k = 10  # Number of independent variables in the model
adjusted_r2 = 1 - ((1 - r2) * (n - 1) / (n - k - 1))
print("Adjusted R-squared:", adjusted_r2)
```

Adjusted R-squared: 0.38242363001960145

An adjusted R-squared score of 0.38 suggests that the regression model explains about 38% of the variation in the dependent variable, given the complexity of the model and the number of independent variables. Further analysis and refinement of the model is required to achieve a higher degree of explanation and improve the overall performance of the regression model.

Summary

This chapter has specifically focused on evaluating the performance of classification and regression models using various metrics.

For the classification models, we explored a range of performance appraisal measures. Accuracy, which measures the proportion of correctly classified instances, has been discussed as a fundamental metric. Precision, recall, and F1 score were explored to assess the model's ability to correctly identify positives, detect all positives, and provide a balanced assessment of precision and recall. The concept of confusion matrix was introduced, allowing us to have an overview of true positives, true negatives, false positives and false negatives. Finally, AUC (Area Under the Curve) and ROC (Receiver Operating Characteristic) were covered as metrics to assess the performance of the model across different thresholds.

Moving on to regression models, we explored performance evaluation measures specific to regression tasks. Mean Squared Error (MSE) was introduced as a metric that measures the mean squared difference between predicted and actual values. The root mean squared error (RMSE) provided a more interpretable metric by taking the square root of MSE. The mean absolute error (MAE) quantified the mean absolute difference between the predicted and actual values. The R-squared, also known as the coefficient of determination assessed how well the model explains the variation in the dependent variable. Finally, adjusted R-squared was introduced as a modified version of R-squared that considers the number of independent variables and adjusts the quality of the fit measure accordingly.

Chapter 5: Naive Bayes

In this chapter, we will dive into the fascinating world of Naive Bayes, a powerful and probabilistic machine learning algorithm widely used in various fields. Naive Bayes offers an elegant and efficient approach to classification tasks, which makes it particularly useful in applications such as text categorization, spam filtering, sentiment analysis, etc. This chapter provides a comprehensive introduction to Naive Bayes, including its principles, features, and applications in real-world scenarios.

Introduction

Naive Bayes is built on Bayes' theorem, a fundamental concept in probability theory. This theorem allows us to estimate the probability of a particular event given the observed evidence. Naive Bayes algorithms extend Bayes' theorem to solve classification problems by estimating the probability of a class label given observed features. The key assumption in Naive Bayes is the "naive" assumption of feature independence, which simplifies the modelling process. Although this assumption is not valid in all cases, Naive Bayes has demonstrated remarkable efficiency in many applications.

The mathematical formula behind Naive Bayes is to calculate the posterior probability of a class label given features using prior probability and likelihood. The posterior probability represents the likelihood of a particular class label given the observed evidence. It is calculated using Bayes' theorem and can be further simplified by assuming feature independence.

The formula can be expressed as follows:

$$P(y \mid x_1, x_2, ..., x_n) = (P(y) * P(x_1 \mid y) * P(x_2 \mid y) * ... * P(x_n \mid y)) / P(x_1, x_2, ..., x_n)$$

In this formula, P(y) represents the prior probability of the class label and P(xi | y) represents the probability of observing feature xi given the class label y. By calculating the posterior probabilities for each class label, Naive Bayes determines the most likely class label for a given set of features.

A real business problem where Naive Bayes can be used is spam filtering. The task is to classify incoming emails as spam or legitimate based on their content and characteristics. Naive Bayes can be applied in this scenario by training a model on a labelled dataset of emails, where features are derived from email content, sender information, and other relevant attributes.

The trained Naive Bayes model can then classify new incoming emails as spam or legitimate based on probabilities calculated using the observed characteristics. This enables efficient and accurate filtering of emails, thereby reducing the spam load on users' inboxes.

How to Identify if your problem can be solved using Naive Bayes algorithms?

Identifying a problem suitable for Naive Bayes involves considering the nature of the data and the problem itself. Naive Bayes works well when the feature independence assumption holds reasonably well. It is especially effective in scenarios with a large number of features and relatively small training datasets. Naive Bayes also tends to work well with textual data and categorical features. By examining the characteristics of the problem and the available data, one can determine if Naive Bayes is an appropriate choice.

Naive Bayes Algorithms

In this section, we will explore the following Naive Bayes algorithms:

- Gaussian Naive Bayes: This algorithm is well suited for continuous features that follow a Gaussian or normal distribution. It assumes that the features of each class label are normally distributed, which allows it to estimate the mean and standard deviation to calculate the likelihood probabilities.

- Multinomial Naive Bayes: Designed for discrete features that represent counts or frequencies, such as word occurrences in text classification tasks. This algorithm assumes a multinomial distribution for the features and estimates the probabilities based on the frequency of occurrence in each class label.

- Bernoulli Naive Bayes: Suitable for binary or boolean features that only take two values, such as the presence or absence of certain attributes. It assumes a Bernoulli distribution for the features and estimates the probabilities based on the presence or absence of the features in each class label.

Each Naive Bayes algorithm works on the fundamentals of Bayes' theorem and feature independence, but they differ in their underlying probability distributions and how they handle specific types of features. This diversity allows practitioners to choose the most appropriate variant for their classification tasks, depending on the nature of the data and the problem to be solved.

By the end of this chapter, readers will have a complete understanding of Naive Bayes algorithms and their versatility in classification tasks. They will be empowered to apply these algorithms to real-world problems, leveraging their probabilistic foundations to make accurate predictions and gain valuable insights from their data.

Gaussian Naive Bayes

Gaussian Naive Bayes is a variation of the Naive Bayes algorithm that excels at handling continuous features that follow a Gaussian or normal distribution. It is a powerful and efficient classification algorithm widely used in various fields, such as medical diagnosis, sentiment analysis, and fraud detection. Gaussian Naive Bayes exploits the probabilistic framework of Bayes' theorem and the feature independence assumption to make accurate predictions based on observed continuous features.

Gaussian Naive Bayes works by estimating the probability of class labels given observed features. It assumes that the features in each class label are normally distributed, allowing the mean and standard deviation to be estimated for each feature in each class. The algorithm calculates the likelihood probabilities assuming the features are conditionally independent given the class label. These probabilities, along with the prior probabilities of the class labels, are combined using Bayes' theorem to determine the most likely class label for a given set of features.

Gaussian Naive Bayes is particularly well suited to data that follows a Gaussian or normal distribution. Continuous characteristics such as age, height, temperature, and other measurable quantities often exhibit this distribution. When the feature independence assumption holds reasonably well and the features can be reasonably approximated by a normal distribution, Gaussian Naive Bayes can provide robust and accurate classification results.

An example of a real business problem where Gaussian Naive Bayes can be used is Medical Diagnostics. Suppose we have a dataset that contains various patient attributes such as age, blood pressure, cholesterol level, and symptoms along with the corresponding diagnoses of a particular disease. Gaussian Naive Bayes can be used to predict the likelihood that a patient will have the disease based on the continuous characteristics observed. By modelling the features as normally distributed in each class label, the algorithm can provide valuable information and help healthcare professionals diagnose diseases more accurately and efficiently.

> **How to Identify if your problem can be solved using Gaussian Naive Bayes?**
>
> Identifying a problem suitable for Gaussian Naive Bayes involves considering the nature of the data and the problem itself. Gaussian Naive Bayes works well when the continuous features in the dataset follow a Gaussian distribution and are approximately independent of each other. By examining the features of the problem, evaluating the feature distribution, and ensuring that the independence assumption is reasonable, one can determine whether Gaussian Naive Bayes is an appropriate choice for the classification problem in question.

To demonstrate the implementation of Gaussian Naive Bayes using Python, we will use a dataset from the scikit-learn library. Let's start by importing the necessary libraries and loading the dataset:

```
from sklearn.datasets import make_classification
from sklearn.model_selection import train_test_split
from sklearn.naive_bayes import GaussianNB
from sklearn.metrics import accuracy_score

# Generate a synthetic dataset with normally distributed features
X, y = make_classification(n_samples=1000, n_features=4, n_informative=2,
n_redundant=2, random_state=42)

# Split the dataset into training and testing sets
X_train, X_test, y_train, y_test = train_test_split(X, y, test_size=0.2,
random_state=42)
```

Understanding Parameters:

- make_classification: This is a function of the datasets module of scikit-learn that allows us to generate a synthetic classification dataset with specified characteristics.

- n_samples: Total number of samples or instances in the dataset. In this case, we generate 1000 samples.

- n_features: The number of features or independent variables in each sample. Here we have 4 features.

- n_informative: the number of informative features, which are the features that contribute to class separation. In this case, we have 2 informative features.
- n_redundant: the number of redundant features, which correlates with informative features but does not provide additional information. Here we have 2 redundant features.

- random_state: the random seed used to ensure the reproducibility of the generated dataset.

Now let's train and evaluate the Gaussian Naive Bayes classifier on our dataset:

```
# Create an instance of the Gaussian Naive Bayes classifier
gnb = GaussianNB()

# Train the model on the training data
gnb.fit(X_train, y_train)

# Make predictions on the testing data
y_pred = gnb.predict(X_test)

# Calculate the accuracy of the model
accuracy = accuracy_score(y_test, y_pred)
print("Accuracy:", accuracy)
```

Accuracy: 0.84

Multinomial Naive Bayes

Multinomial Naive Bayes is a variation of the Naive Bayes algorithm specifically designed to handle discrete features, such as word occurrences in text classification tasks. It is an algorithm widely used in natural language processing, document classification and spam filtering. Multinomial Naive Bayes exploits the probabilistic framework of Bayes' theorem and the feature independence assumption to make predictions based on the frequency distribution of discrete features.

Multinomial Naive Bayes works by estimating the probability of class labels given observed features. It assumes a multinomial distribution for features, which represents the frequency of occurrence within each class label. The algorithm calculates likelihood probabilities based on the frequency of occurrence of each feature in each class label. It also considers prior probabilities of class labels and combines them with likelihood probabilities using Bayes' theorem to determine the most likely class label for a given set of features.

For example, consider a real business problem where we seek to classify customer reviews as positive, negative, or neutral based on text content. Multinomial Naive Bayes can be used to predict the likelihood that a customer review belongs to each sentiment class based on the frequency distribution of words in the reviews. By modelling the discrete features as numbers and assuming their independence, the algorithm can efficiently rank customer reviews, allowing businesses to gain insight into customer sentiment and make informed decisions accordingly.

> **How to Identify if your problem can be solved using Multinomial Naive Bayes?**

> Identifying a problem suitable for Multinomial Naive Bayes involves considering the nature of the data and the problem itself. Multinomial Naive Bayes works well when features are discrete and can be represented as numbers or frequencies. By examining the features of the data, evaluating the type of features, and ensuring that the assumption of feature independence is reasonable, one can determine whether Multinomial Naive Bayes is an appropriate choice to solve the classification problem at hand.

To demonstrate the implementation of Multinomial Naive Bayes using Python, we will use a dataset from the scikit-learn library. Let's start by importing the necessary libraries and loading the dataset:

```python
from sklearn.datasets import fetch_20newsgroups
from sklearn.feature_extraction.text import CountVectorizer
from sklearn.model_selection import train_test_split
from sklearn.naive_bayes import MultinomialNB
from sklearn.metrics import accuracy_score

# Load the dataset
data = fetch_20newsgroups(subset='all')

# Extract the features from the dataset
vectorizer = CountVectorizer()
X = vectorizer.fit_transform(data.data)
y = data.target

# Split the dataset into training and testing sets
X_train, X_test, y_train, y_test = train_test_split(X, y, test_size=0.2, random_state=42)
```

In the code above, we used the CountVectorizer class which you may not be familiar with. This class converts textual data into a matrix of token counts, where each row corresponds to a document and each column represents the count of a specific word in that document. This step is essential to transform the textual data into a format suitable for Multinomial Naive Bayes.

Now, let's train and evaluate the Multinomial Naive Bayes classifier on our dataset:

```python
# Create an instance of the Multinomial Naive Bayes classifier
mnb = MultinomialNB()

# Train the model on the training data
mnb.fit(X_train, y_train)

# Make predictions on the testing data
y_pred = mnb.predict(X_test)

# Calculate the accuracy of the model
accuracy = accuracy_score(y_test, y_pred)
print("Accuracy:", accuracy)
```

Accuracy: 0.8503978779840848

Bernoulli Naive Bayes

Bernoulli Naive Bayes is a classification algorithm that belongs to the Naive Bayes family. It is specially designed to work with binary entity variables, where each entity represents the presence or absence of a particular attribute. In this algorithm, we assume that the features are conditionally independent given the class label, and we use Bayes' theorem to calculate the probabilities of the different classes.

The Bernoulli Naive Bayes algorithm process has several steps. First, it starts by extracting binary features from the dataset, where each feature represents the presence or absence of a specific attribute or condition. Next, the algorithm calculates the prior probabilities of each class in the training dataset, which reflect the probability of encountering a particular class. It then estimates the probabilities of the binary features within each class, determining the probability of a feature being present or absent based on a class.

Using Bayes' theorem, the algorithm combines class priors and feature probabilities to calculate posterior probabilities. These posterior probabilities represent the probability of a particular class given the presence or absence of certain characteristics. Finally, when classifying new instances, Bernoulli Naive Bayes calculates the probabilities of each class for the given features and assigns the class with the highest probability as the predicted class for the instance.

Bernoulli Naive Bayes is suitable for datasets with binary features, where each feature is represented by a 0 or 1, indicating its absence or presence. It works well with categorical data that can be transformed into binary forms, such as textual data where the presence or absence of specific words is taken into account.

Bernoulli Naive Bayes can be applied to various business problems. For example, it can be used in the classification of email spam. By considering the presence or absence of specific words or patterns in an email, Bernoulli Naive Bayes can predict whether an email is spam or not. It analyzes the binary characteristics of the email, such as the occurrence of certain keywords or the presence of suspicious patterns, to perform the classification.

> **How to Identify if your problem can be solved using Bernoulli Naive Bayes?**
>
> To determine if Bernoulli Naive Bayes is suitable for a problem, consider the nature of the data and whether the features can be represented as binary values. If the dataset consists of binary or categorical features and you want to predict a categorical outcome, Bernoulli Naive Bayes might be a good choice. Also, if the features are conditionally independent given that the class label assumption holds reasonably well for the problem at hand, Bernoulli Naive Bayes can provide accurate predictions.

Here is an implementation of the Bernoulli Naive Bayes algorithm using Python:

```python
from sklearn.datasets import make_classification
from sklearn.model_selection import train_test_split
from sklearn.naive_bayes import BernoulliNB
```

```python
from sklearn.metrics import accuracy_score

# Generate a synthetic dataset with 1000 samples and 20 features
X, y = make_classification(n_samples=1000, n_features=20, n_informative=10,
n_redundant=5, random_state=42)

# Split the dataset into training and testing sets
X_train, X_test, y_train, y_test = train_test_split(X, y, test_size=0.2,
random_state=42)

# Create a Bernoulli Naive Bayes classifier object
clf = BernoulliNB()

# Train the classifier on the training data
clf.fit(X_train, y_train)

# Make predictions on the test data
y_pred = clf.predict(X_test)
```

Advantages & Disadvantages of Naive Bayes Algorithm

The naive Bayes algorithm offers several advantages in machine learning. First, it is computationally efficient and scales well to large datasets. It can handle a large number of features and performs well even when the independence assumption is violated to some degree. Naive Bayes is particularly effective when it comes to text classification tasks and has demonstrated good performance in spam filtering and sentiment analysis. Moreover, it requires a small amount of training data to estimate the parameters accurately. The algorithm is also relatively simple to implement and interpret, making it accessible to beginners and experienced practitioners alike.

Despite its strengths, Naive Bayes has some limitations to consider. A major drawback is its strong assumption of feature independence, which may not be true in some real-world scenarios. Therefore, the model may produce suboptimal results when confronted with highly correlated characteristics. Additionally, Naive Bayes assumes that each feature contributes equally to the final classification, which may not always be accurate. This can lead to a loss of discriminating power and lower accuracy compared to more sophisticated algorithms. Another limitation is the "zero frequency problem", where a feature value present in the test set but absent from the training set can cause the model to assign a zero probability, resulting in incorrect predictions. Finally, Naive Bayes is considered a "naive" algorithm because it neglects the relationships between features, which can limit its effectiveness in some complex classification tasks.

Summary

In this chapter, we explored the Naive Bayes algorithm and its different implementations. We started by understanding the concept of Naive Bayes and its underlying assumption of feature independence. We then looked at the different Naive Bayes algorithms: Gaussian Naive Bayes, Multinomial Naive Bayes and Bernoulli Naive Bayes.

Gaussian Naive Bayes is suitable for continuous or real-valued data, Multinomial Naive Bayes works well with discrete data, and Bernoulli Naive Bayes is ideal for binary or Boolean characteristics. We have discussed the advantages of Naive Bayes, such as its computational efficiency, scalability to large datasets, and efficiency in text classification tasks. However, we also highlighted its limitations, including the strong assumption of feature independence and potentially suboptimal performance in cases of correlated features.

Chapter 6: Support Vector Machines

In this chapter, we will explore the concept of support vector machines and delve into its various aspects. We'll cover topics like the intuition behind SVM, how it works, the different types of SVM algorithms, the mathematical formulation, and the pros and cons of SVM. Additionally, we will discuss practical implementations of SVM using popular Python libraries and provide real-world examples to demonstrate its applications in solving complex business problems.

Introduction

Support Vector Machines (SVM) is a powerful machine learning algorithm that excels at solving complex classification and regression problems. It is widely used in various fields including finance, healthcare, and image recognition. SVMs are known for their ability to find optimal decision bounds in high-dimensional feature spaces, which makes them effective for both linearly separable and nonlinearly separable datasets.

The central idea behind SVM is to find the best hyperplane that separates data into different classes while maximizing the margin or distance between classes. SVM achieves this by transforming the input data into a higher dimensional space using a kernel function. In this new space, SVM finds the hyperplane that maximizes the margin between classes. The data points closest to the hyperplane, known as support vectors, play a crucial role in defining the decision boundary and overall model performance.

The mathematical formulation of SVM is to find the optimal values of the model parameters to minimize the classification error and maximize the margin. Given a set of training data, SVM aims to solve a constrained optimization problem, commonly known as a primal problem, using techniques such as Lagrange multipliers.

The decision function for SVM can be represented by the equation $f(x) = sign(w^T x + b)$, where w represents the weights, x is the input feature vector, and b is the bias term.

An example of a real business problem where SVM can be used is credit card fraud detection. The problem is to classify credit card transactions as fraudulent or genuine. SVM can learn from historical transaction data and identify patterns that distinguish fraudulent transactions from legitimate transactions. By training an SVM model on features such as transaction amount, location, and time, it can effectively predict and flag potential fraud cases, allowing businesses to take immediate action and protect their customers.

The Concept of Decision Boundary in SVM

In support vector machines (SVM), the decision boundary plays a crucial role in separating different classes within the data set. It represents the line or area that determines the classification of new data points. The decision boundary is derived based on the training data and is designed to maximize the margin, which is the distance between the decision boundary and the closest data points in each class. The SVM algorithm aims to find the optimal decision boundary that achieves the best trade-off between classification accuracy and generalization to unseen data.

Consider a simple example of a binary classification problem. Imagine a dataset where classes are represented by two distinct groups of points on a two-dimensional graph. The x-axis and the y-axis represent different features and each point is labeled as class 0 or class 1. The decision boundary, in this case, is a line that separates the two classes. Data points falling on one side of the decision boundary are classified as class 0, while those on the other side are classified as class 1.

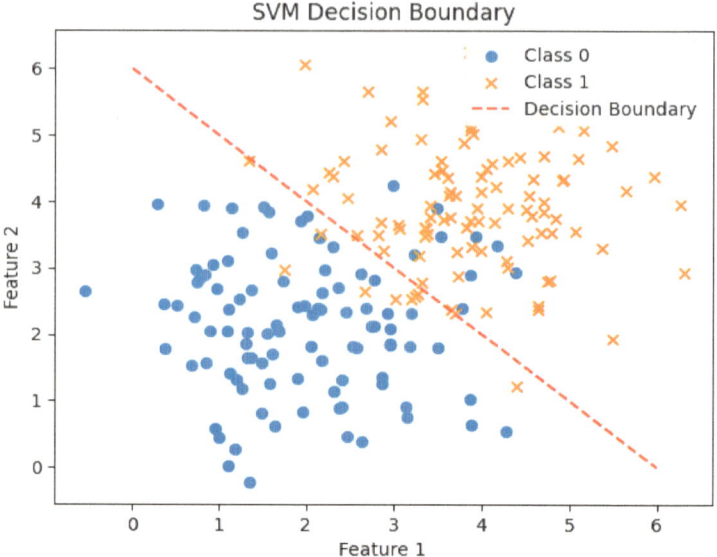

In this example, the decision boundary is a straight line that separates the two classes. Any new data point falling on one side of the decision boundary will be classified in the corresponding class. The goal of SVM is to find the decision boundary that maximizes the margin, allowing better generalization and improved accuracy when classifying unseen data.

> **How to Identify if your problem can be solved using Support Vector Machines?**
>
> Support vector machines are suitable for both binary and multi-class classification problems. They work well when there is a clear separation between classes or when the dataset is not easily linearly separable. SVMs can handle large feature spaces and are effective in scenarios where the number of features is greater than

the number of samples. Additionally, SVMs are robust to noise in the data and have the ability to handle large datasets efficiently. When dealing with classification problems that require precise decision bounds and good generalization performance, SVMs can be a suitable choice.

Implementation of SVM for Classification

Here is a Support Vector Machines (SVM) implementation using Python for solving classification problems on the popular Iris data:

```python
import numpy as np
import matplotlib.pyplot as plt
from sklearn.datasets import load_iris
from sklearn.model_selection import train_test_split
from sklearn.svm import SVC
import plotly.graph_objects as go

# Load the Iris dataset
iris = load_iris()
X = iris.data[:, :2]  # Consider only the first two features for visualization
y = iris.target

# Split the dataset into training and testing sets
X_train, X_test, y_train, y_test = train_test_split(X, y, test_size=0.2, random_state=42)

# Create an instance of the SVM classifier
svm = SVC(kernel='linear')

# Train the SVM classifier
svm.fit(X_train, y_train)

# Evaluate the model on the test set
accuracy = svm.score(X_test, y_test)
print("Accuracy:", accuracy)
```

Accuracy: 0.9

In the given code snippet, svm = SVC(kernel='linear') initializes an instance of the Support Vector Machine (SVM) classifier. The SVM classifier is configured to use a linear kernel, which means it assumes a linear decision boundary between classes. The kernel determines the type of decision boundary that the SVM will learn.

By specifying kernel='linear', we instruct the SVM classifier to use a linear kernel, which is suitable for problems where the data may be separated by a straight line in feature space. The linear kernel computes the decision boundary as a hyperplane, a high-dimensional plane that separates data points of different classes.

The choice of the kernel depends on the nature of the data and the problem treated. In this case, we use a linear kernel because we want to learn a linear decision boundary between classes. However, SVM also supports other kernel functions such as polynomial and radial basis function (RBF), which can capture nonlinear decision bounds in more complex datasets.

Now here's how to visualize the decision boundary of the SVM model we trained above:

```
# Define the decision boundary
x_min, x_max = X[:, 0].min() - 1, X[:, 0].max() + 1
y_min, y_max = X[:, 1].min() - 1, X[:, 1].max() + 1
h = 0.02  # Step size for the meshgrid
xx, yy = np.meshgrid(np.arange(x_min, x_max, h), np.arange(y_min, y_max, h))

# Predict the class labels for the meshgrid points
Z = svm.predict(np.c_[xx.ravel(), yy.ravel()])
Z = Z.reshape(xx.shape)


# Visualize the data points and the decision boundary using Plotly
fig = go.Figure()
fig.add_trace(go.Scatter(x=X[:, 0], y=X[:, 1], mode='markers',
                         marker=dict(color=y, colorscale='RdYlBu', size=8),
                         text=[iris.target_names[i] for i in y]))

fig.add_trace(go.Contour(x=np.arange(x_min, x_max, h),
                         y=np.arange(y_min, y_max, h), z=Z, showscale=False,
opacity=0.8))
fig.update_layout(title='SVM Decision Boundary (Iris Dataset)',
                  xaxis_title='Sepal Length (cm)',
                  yaxis_title='Sepal Width (cm)', showlegend=False)
fig.show()
```

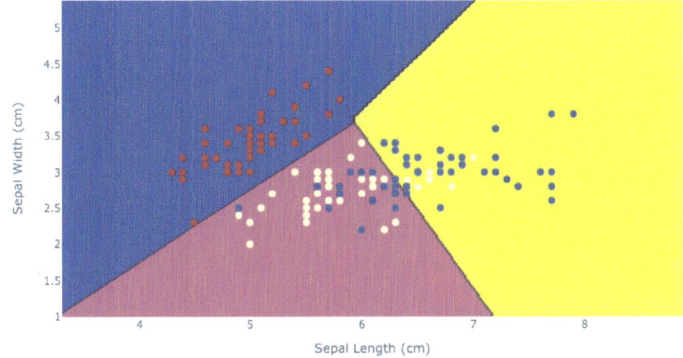

SVM Decision Boundary (Iris Dataset)

In the image above, the scatter plot represents data points from the Iris dataset, where each point is coloured according to its corresponding class label. The decision boundary is represented by the black line that separates the different classes. This line acts as the boundary where the SVM algorithm classifies the data points into their respective classes. Any new data points falling on one side of the decision boundary will be classified in one class, while points on the other side will be classified in the other class. The decision boundary aims to maximize the margin between the two classes, ensuring the best separation.

SVM for Regression

While solving a regression problem, support vector machines (SVMs) aims to find a hyperplane that best fits the given data points while minimizing the error between the predicted and actual target values. The key idea behind SVM regression is to maximize the margin between the hyperplane and the nearest data points.

Unlike classification tasks, where SVM aims to find a hyperplane that separates different classes, SVM for regression seeks to find a hyperplane that crosses as many data points as possible while controlling the width of the margin. The hyperplane is chosen so that the sum of the distances between the data points and the hyperplane is minimized, allowing accurate predictions of the target variable. To do this, SVM uses a loss function that penalizes the distance between the predicted and actual target values. The objective is to find the hyperplane which minimizes this loss function while satisfying certain constraints. The loss function used in SVM regression is typically epsilon-insensitive loss, where errors below a specified threshold (epsilon) are not penalized.

SVM for regression involves solving a quadratic programming problem to find the optimal values for the coefficients and the bias term in the hyperplane equation. The mathematical formulation of SVM regression is to minimize the objective function, which includes the loss function, the regularization term, and the hyperplane weights.

Here is an example of using SVM for regression:

Dataset Download Link:
https://statso.io/usd-inr-conversion-rate-case-study/

```
import pandas as pd
from sklearn.model_selection import train_test_split
from sklearn.svm import SVR
from sklearn.metrics import r2_score

# Load the dataset
data = pd.read_csv('INR-USD.csv')
data = data.dropna()
# Split the data into features (X) and target variable (y)
X = data[['Open', 'High', 'Low', 'Adj Close', 'Volume']]
y = data['Close']

# Split the data into training and testing sets
X_train, X_test, y_train, y_test = train_test_split(X, y, test_size=0.2, random_state=42)
# Train the SVM regression model
svm = SVR(kernel='linear')
svm.fit(X_train, y_train)

# Make predictions on the testing set
```

```python
y_pred = svm.predict(X_test)
# Evaluate the model
r2 = r2_score(y_test, y_pred)
print('R-squared Score:', r2)
```

R-squared Score: 0.99998656474119

Now here's how to look at the actual and predicted values:

```python
import plotly.graph_objects as go

fig = go.Figure()
fig.add_trace(go.Scatter(x=y_test, y=y_pred, mode='markers', name='Data Points'))
fig.add_trace(go.Scatter(x=y_test, y=y_test, mode='lines', name='Perfect Prediction'))
fig.update_layout(title='USD - INR Closing Rate: Actual vs Predicted',
                  xaxis_title='Actual Values',
                  yaxis_title='Predicted Values')
fig.show()
```

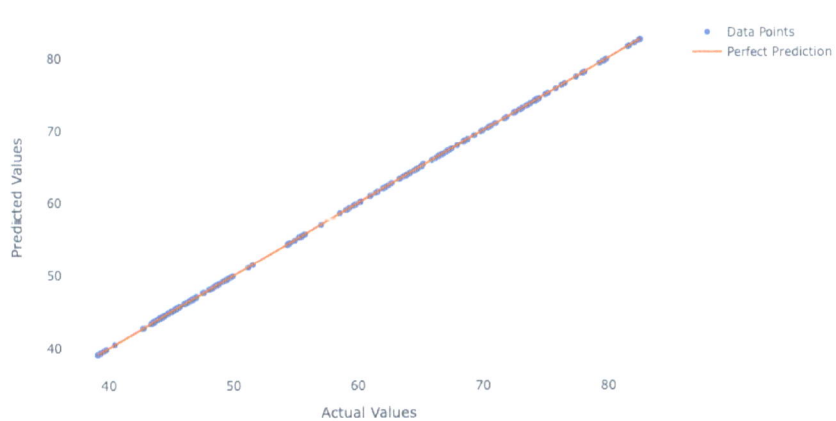

In the image above, the scatter plot represents the actual and forecasted values of the USD - INR closing rates. Each data point on the graph corresponds to an actual value on the x-axis and its corresponding predicted value on the y-axis. Points are represented by markers on the plot.

The line that goes from the lower left corner to the upper right corner of the graph represents the perfect prediction line. This line indicates the scenario where the predicted values exactly match the actual values.

Looking at the plot, you can see that all the data points fall perfectly on this line. This implies that the predicted values align closely with the actual values, indicating a high level of accuracy in the regression model predictions. The fact that the data points are closely clustered along the perfect prediction line suggests that the model performed exceptionally well in estimating USD-INR close rates.

Advantages & Disadvantages of SVM

Support vector machines (SVMs) offer several advantages in machine learning. First, SVM performs well in high-dimensional spaces, which makes it suitable for complex problems with a large number of features. Second, it is efficient for handling both linearly separable and nonlinearly separable data using kernel functions. Moreover, SVM is robust against overfitting and can generalize well to new data.

However, SVM has some limitations. This can be computationally expensive and memory intensive, especially for large datasets. SVM also requires a careful selection of kernel hyperparameters and functions to achieve optimal performance. Finally, SVM may not work properly when the dataset is unbalanced or contains overlapping classes. Therefore, it is important to consider the specific characteristics of the problem and the dataset when deciding to use SVM.

Summary

In this chapter, we looked at Support Vector Machines (SVM), a powerful machine learning algorithm widely used for classification and regression tasks.

Next, we covered the SVM implementation for classification, where the algorithm seeks to find the best hyperplane to classify data points into distinct classes. We discussed the different kernels used in SVM, such as linear, polynomial, and radial basis functions (RBFs), which allow SVM to handle separable data in a nonlinear way.

Moving on to regression, we explored how SVM can be adapted to solve regression problems by fitting a hyperplane that approximates the relationship between input features and target variables. We presented an implementation of SVM for regression using real-world data, highlighting the steps involved and the parameters used to obtain accurate predictions.

In conclusion, SVM is a versatile class of algorithms that excel in classification and regression tasks. Its ability to find optimal decision boundaries and adapt to different types of data makes it a valuable tool in various fields.

Chapter 7: Decision Trees & Ensemble Methods

In this chapter, we will explore the fascinating world of decision trees and ensemble methods. Decision trees are powerful and intuitive models that learn decision rules from data, allowing us to make informed predictions or classifications. We'll dive into the inner workings of decision trees, understand how they make decisions, and explore their benefits and limitations. Additionally, we'll dive into ensemble methods, which combine multiple decision trees to create more robust and accurate models. By the end of this chapter, you will have a complete understanding of decision trees and ensemble methods and how they can be applied in various real-world scenarios.

Introduction

Decision trees are powerful models that learn decision rules from data, allowing us to make informed predictions or classifications. They are widely used in various fields due to their simplicity, interpretability, and ability to handle both categorical and numerical data.

Decision trees work by recursively dividing data based on different attributes to create a tree structure of decision nodes and leaf nodes. At each decision node, the algorithm evaluates a specific feature and determines the optimal distribution based on a criterion such as information gain or Gini impurity. The splitting process continues until a stopping criterion is met, such as reaching a maximum depth or a minimum number of samples at a node.

Let's understand the process of Decision Trees using an example. Suppose you are a bank that wants to determine if a person is likely to be approved for a loan based on their credit score. You collected data on past loan applicants, including their credit scores and whether their loan applications were approved. Below is how Decision trees will solve this problem.

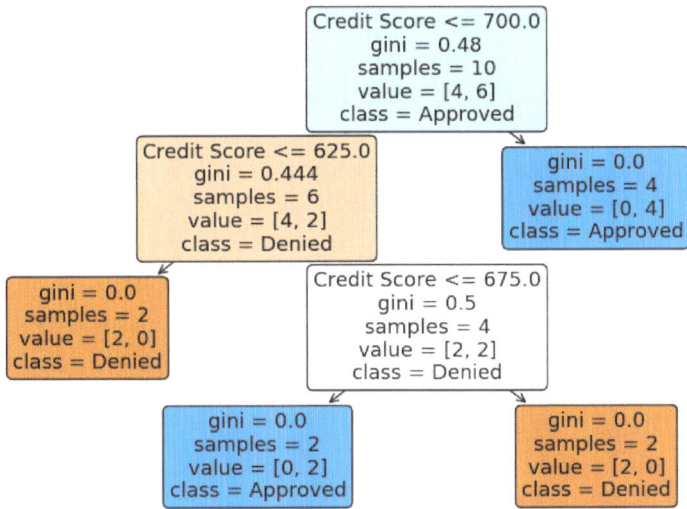

In this problem, the decision tree algorithm will start with a "root" node representing the first question, such as whether a person's credit score is above or below a certain threshold.

Depending on the answer, the algorithm follows branches to subsequent questions, such as income level or employment status, until a "leaf" node is reached. The leaf node represents a decision, such as predicting whether to approve or deny a loan based on input characteristics.

So, a decision tree algorithm is like a flowchart that makes decisions based on a series of questions and answers. It starts at a "root" node with a question, branches to subsequent questions based on the answers, and finally reaches a "leaf" node representing a decision.

How to Identify if your problem can be solved using Decision Trees?

Decision trees are well suited to various types of problems. They excel in situations where interpretability and transparency are important, as they provide explicit decision rules that can be easily understood by humans. Decision trees are particularly useful when dealing with categorical entities or when the relationships between entities and the target variable are not linear. Additionally, decision trees are good at handling unbalanced datasets and can handle missing values or outliers with proper preprocessing. If you have a dataset with these characteristics, decision trees can be an excellent choice for solving your problem.

Decision Trees Algorithms & Ensemble Methods

Here are all the decision trees algorithms and ensemble methods that we will be covering in this chapter:

- CART (Classification and Regression Trees): CART is a versatile decision tree algorithm that can be used for both classification and regression tasks. It uses binary splitting to split data based on feature thresholds, creating a tree structure. For classification, CART uses impurity or Gini entropy as the division criterion to maximize the purity of each node. In regression, it aims to minimize the mean squared error at each node.

- ID3 (Iterative Dichotomiser 3): ID3 is a decision tree algorithm mainly used for classification tasks. It follows a top-down and greedy approach to build the tree by selecting the best attribute at each step based on the information gained. Information gain measures the reduction in entropy or uncertainty achieved by separating a particular attribute. ID3 supports categorical attributes and can handle missing values, but it may struggle with continuous features.

- C4.5: C4.5 is an extension of the ID3 algorithm which addresses some of its limitations. Like ID3, C4.5 is used for classification tasks. It introduces the concept of attribute-specific payoff ratios, which explains the bias in favour of attributes with a large number of distinct values. C4.5 also handles categorical and continuous attributes and incorporates techniques to handle missing values.

- Ensemble Methods: The ensemble methods (Random Forests and Gradient Boosting) in decision trees offer several advantages. They are robust against overfitting because combining multiple models helps to balance out the biases of individual models. They also handle high-dimensional data well and can capture complex interactions between features. Ensemble methods are versatile and can be used for both classification and regression tasks. However, they may require more computational resources and longer training times compared to individual decision trees.

The Concept of Ensemble Methods in Decision Trees

Ensemble methods in decision trees refer to the technique of combining multiple individual decision trees to make more accurate and robust predictions. The idea behind ensemble methods is that by leveraging the collective wisdom of multiple models, we can overcome the limitations of individual decision trees and improve overall prediction performance.

There are several popular ensemble methods used in conjunction with decision trees, including Random Forest and Gradient Boosting. In Random Forest, a collection of decision trees is constructed using bootstrap sampling and randomness. Each tree makes predictions independently, and the final prediction is determined by aggregating the predictions from all the trees. This ensemble approach helps reduce overfitting, handle noisy data, and capture a wider range of patterns in the data.

Gradient Boosting, on the other hand, is an ensemble method that builds decision trees sequentially. Each subsequent tree is constructed to correct faults or errors made by previous trees. The algorithm optimizes a loss function using gradient descent, updating the tree iteratively to minimize residuals. By combining predictions from multiple trees, Gradient Boosting achieves greater predictive accuracy and captures complex relationships in the data.

Now let's explore Decision tree algorithms and ensemble methods in detail one by one.

CART

CART (Classification and Regression Trees) is a popular algorithm used in machine learning models based on decision trees. It is widely used for classification and regression tasks and is known for its simplicity and interpretability. CART builds binary decision trees by recursively partitioning data based on input feature values, to create homogeneous subsets that are purer in terms of the target variable.

To create the decision tree, CART recursively splits the data based on the selected entity and the split point, creating child nodes that represent the resulting subsets.

This process continues until a stopping criterion is met, such as reaching a maximum depth or a minimum number of samples in a leaf node. The final decision tree represents a series of binary splits that rank or predict the target variable based on the input characteristics.

An example of a real business problem where CART in decision trees can be used is credit risk assessment. Given a dataset of credit applicants with various attributes such as income, debt, credit history, and employment status, CART can create a decision tree that classifies applicants as low-risk or high-risk.

We will use the breast cancer dataset available in the scikit-learn library to demonstrate the implementation of CART and other algorithms in decision trees using Python.

This dataset contains features calculated from breast mass images, and the task is to classify tumours as malignant or benign.

Here is the step-by-step process for implementing CART in decision trees:

Step 1: Import the necessary libraries and load the dataset

```
from sklearn.datasets import load_breast_cancer
from sklearn.model_selection import train_test_split
from sklearn.tree import DecisionTreeClassifier
from sklearn import tree

# Load the breast cancer dataset
data = load_breast_cancer()
X = data.data
y = data.target
```

Step 2: Divide the dataset into training and test sets

```python
X_train, X_test, y_train, y_test = train_test_split(X, y, test_size=0.2, random_state=42)
```

Step 3: Create an instance of DecisionTreeClassifier and fit the model to the training data

```python
clf = DecisionTreeClassifier()
clf.fit(X_train, y_train)
```

Step 4: Make predictions on the test set

```python
y_pred = clf.predict(X_test)
```

Step 5: Evaluate the Model's Performance

```python
from sklearn.metrics import accuracy_score

accuracy = accuracy_score(y_test, y_pred)
print("Accuracy:", accuracy)
```

Accuracy: 0.9298245614035088

You can visualize the decision-making process of your model using the code below:

```python
import graphviz

dot_data = tree.export_graphviz(clf, out_file=None,
                                feature_names=data.feature_names,
                                class_names=data.target_names,
                                filled=True, rounded=True,
                                special_characters=True)

graph = graphviz.Source(dot_data)

# Save and open the decision tree as a PDF or image
graph.render("decision_tree", view=True)
```

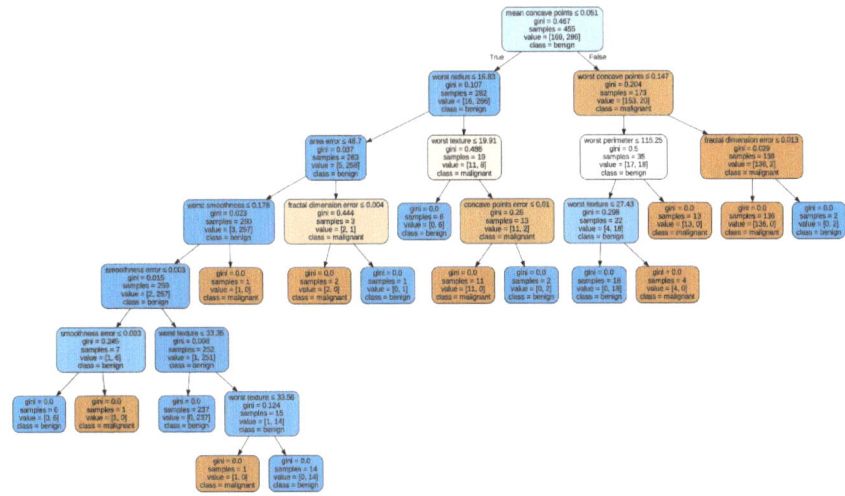

ID3

ID3 (Iterative Dichotomiser 3) is an algorithm used to build decision trees. It is one of the popular and widely used approaches for building decision trees. The ID3 algorithm follows a top-down and greedy strategy to build the tree by selecting the most informative attribute at each step.

Here's how ID3 works in decision trees:

- The ID3 algorithm starts with the complete dataset at the root of the tree.

- It selects the attribute that provides the most information gain or impurity reduction as the root node.

- The dataset is then partitioned based on the selected attribute, creating separate branches for each possible value.

- The process is repeated recursively for each partitioned subset of data, taking into account the remaining attributes, until the tree is completely built.

- The algorithm stops when all instances belong to the same class or when there are no more attributes left to split.

Let's understand how ID3 will help you with the help of an example. Suppose we have a dataset containing customer information including age, income, and purchase history, and we want to predict whether a customer will purchase a specific product.

Using the ID3 algorithm, we can build a decision tree that learns patterns in the data and makes predictions based on customer attributes.

This decision tree can be used in various business areas, such as marketing campaigns, where it can help identify the potential target audience for a product or service.

To train a machine learning model using ID3 in decision trees, you just need to set the criterion as "entropy" as shown below:

```
clf = DecisionTreeClassifier(criterion='entropy')
clf.fit(X_train, y_train)

y_pred = clf.predict(X_test)
accuracy = accuracy_score(y_test, y_pred)
print("Accuracy:", accuracy)
```

Accuracy: 0.956140350877193

Here's the decision process of the ID3 algorithm on the same problem:

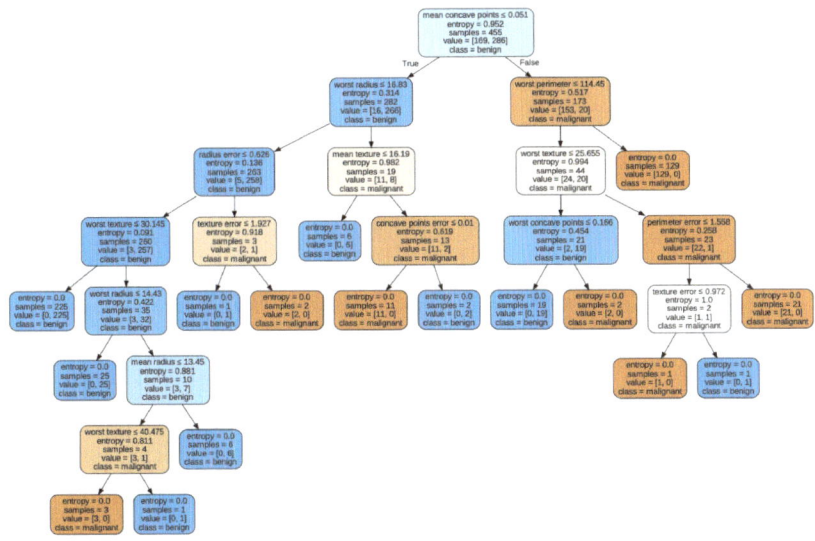

C4.5

C4.5 is an extension of the ID3 algorithm. It improves the limitations of ID3 and introduces additional features to handle continuous attributes and missing data. C4.5 is widely used in machine learning and data mining due to its ability to handle categorical and numeric attributes efficiently.

Here's how C4.5 works in decision trees:

- The C4.5 algorithm follows a process similar to ID3 for building decision trees.

- It starts with the full dataset at the root of the tree and selects the attribute with the highest gain ratio as the root node. The gain ratio takes into account the number of possible outcomes for each attribute.

- C4.5 uses a division criterion called the information gain ratio, which considers both the information gain and the intrinsic information of each attribute.

- To handle continuous attributes, C4.5 performs binary division on the attribute by finding the best threshold that maximizes the information gain.

- C4.5 also handles missing values by considering the weighted information gain for each split.

- The algorithm continues recursively, partitioning the dataset according to the selected attributes and their values until it builds the full decision tree.

To train a machine learning model using C4.5 in decision trees, you just need to set the criterion as "entropy" and the splitter as "best" as shown below:

```
clf = DecisionTreeClassifier(criterion='entropy', splitter='best')
clf.fit(X_train, y_train)

y_pred = clf.predict(X_test)
accuracy = accuracy_score(y_test, y_pred)
print("Accuracy:", accuracy)
```

Accuracy: 0.956140350877193

Here's the decision process of the C4.5 algorithm on the same problem:

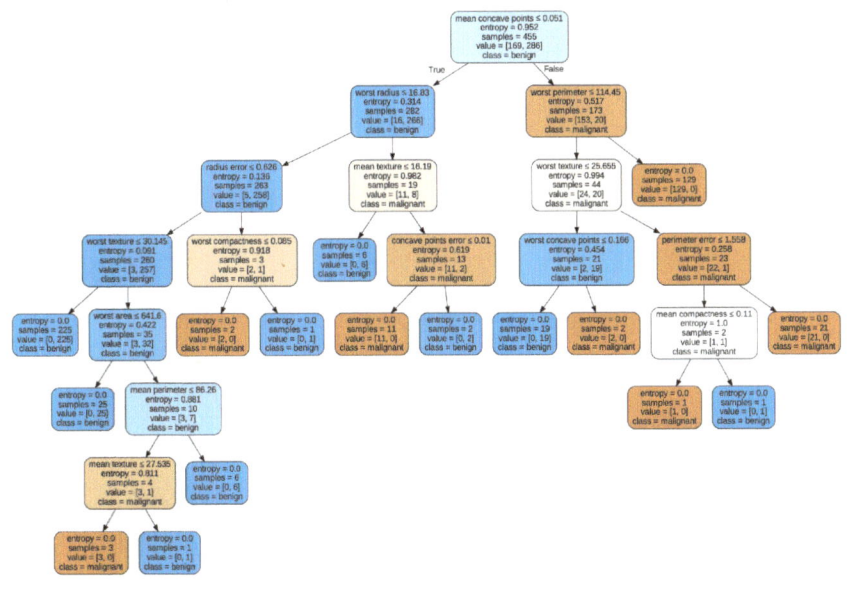

Random Forests

Random Forest is a powerful ensemble learning algorithm that combines multiple decision trees to create a robust and accurate predictive model. It belongs to the family of ensemble methods, which take advantage of the wisdom of multiple models to make better predictions. Random Forest is widely used in machine learning for its ability to handle complex datasets and provide reliable results.

Here's how Random Forest Algorithm works:

- Random Forest builds a set of decision trees using a technique called bootstrap aggregation or bagging. It creates multiple subsets of the original dataset by random sampling with replacement.

- Each subset is then used to train an individual decision tree on a random subset of features. This randomness helps reduce overfitting and increase diversity among trees.

- During the learning process, each decision tree is constructed by selecting the best distribution at each node using criteria such as information gain or Gini impurity.

- When making predictions, Random Forest combines the outputs of all individual trees and uses the vote (for classification) or the mean (for regression) to determine the final prediction.

- Random Forest also introduces the concept of random feature selection. Instead of considering all features at each split, it randomly selects a subset of features, which further improves the diversity and performance of the model.

- The final prediction is based on the majority vote (for classification) or the average (for regression) of the predictions of all the individual trees.

Now let's take an example of how the Random Forest algorithm solves a real-time problem. Suppose a healthcare provider wants to predict a patient's likelihood of readmission within 30 days of discharge. Using Random Forest, the provider can build a predictive model using various patient attributes such as age, medical history, vital signs, and medication use.

Random Forest can handle complex relationships between predictor variables and the target variable, making it effective in identifying patterns and accurately predicting patient readmission risk.

> **How to Identify if your problem can be solved using Random Forests?**
>
> Random Forest is well suited for problems that involve classification and regression tasks. It works especially well when there are complex interactions and non-linear relationships between the entities and the target variable. Additionally, Random Forest can efficiently handle large datasets, high-dimensional data, and missing values. If you have a problem that requires accurate predictions with good generalization abilities and handles different kinds of features, Random Forest is a promising algorithm to consider.

The Concept of Bagging in Random Forests

Bagging, short for Bootstrap Aggregating, is a concept used in Random Forests to create a set of decision trees. This involves creating multiple subsets of the original dataset by random sampling with replacement. Each subset called a bootstrap sample, is used to form an individual decision tree. The idea behind bagging is to introduce diversity among trees by giving them different perspectives of the data.

To better understand the concept of bagging, imagine a dataset with multiple data points scattered across the coordinate plane. Each data point represents an instance with its corresponding features and target value. The x-axis represents one characteristic, while the y-axis represents another characteristic or the target variable.

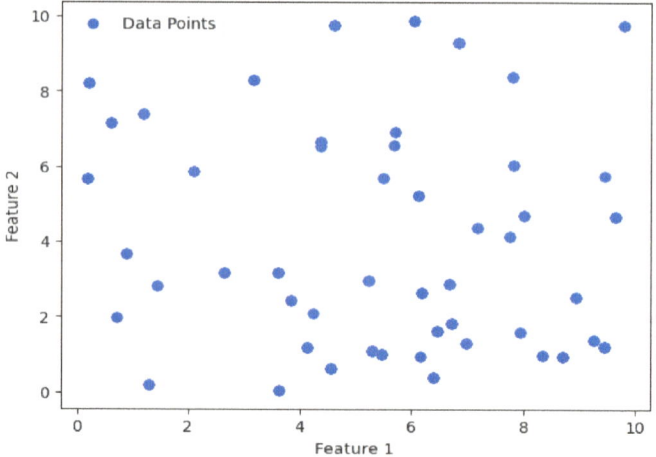

To create a bootstrap sample, we perform random sampling with replacement. This means that for each data point in the original dataset, we randomly select another data point in the dataset, even if it is the same data point. This process is repeated to create a subset of the dataset.

Now imagine creating multiple subsets using this random sampling technique. Each subset has a different combination of data points, capturing different perspectives and variations in the dataset.

With these subsets, we can form individual decision trees. Each decision tree will have its own set of training data, slightly different from the others. This diversity is key to the power of bagging in Random Forest.

By combining predictions from all individual decision trees, Random Forest achieves better accuracy and robustness. It reduces the impact of outliers and noise, improves generalization and provides more reliable predictions.

Implementation of Random Forests

Here is an implementation of the Random Forest algorithm for classification on the breast cancer dataset:

```python
from sklearn.ensemble import RandomForestClassifier
from sklearn.datasets import load_breast_cancer
from sklearn.model_selection import train_test_split
from sklearn.metrics import accuracy_score

# Load the breast cancer dataset
data = load_breast_cancer()
X = data.data
y = data.target

# Split the dataset into training and testing sets
X_train, X_test, y_train, y_test = train_test_split(X, y, test_size=0.2, random_state=42)

# Create a Random Forest classifier
rf = RandomForestClassifier(n_estimators=100, random_state=42)

# Train the Random Forest model
rf.fit(X_train, y_train)

# Make predictions on the test set
y_pred = rf.predict(X_test)

# Evaluate the accuracy of the model
accuracy = accuracy_score(y_test, y_pred)
print("Accuracy:", accuracy)
```

Accuracy: 0.9649122807017544

In the above code, the line **rf = RandomForestClassifier(n_estimators=100, random_state=42)** is used to create an instance of the Random Forest classifier.

The n_estimators parameter specifies the number of decision trees to include in the random forest. Increasing the number of estimators can improve model performance, but it also increases computational complexity and training time. The optimal value for n_estimators depends on the dataset and can be determined by experimentation.

The random_state parameter is used to set the random seed for reproducibility. Random forests involve randomness, such as training data sampling and feature selection, which can lead to different model results each time it is run. By setting a random seed, we ensure that the same results can be reproduced if the code is run multiple times with the same seed value.

It is not necessary to specify these parameters each time when implementing random forests, but they are often considered important for reproducibility and control of model behaviour. The choice of values for these parameters depends on the specific problem and dataset. Experimentation and tuning are commonly used to find the optimal values that result in the best model performance.

Gradient Boosting

Gradient Boosting is a powerful ensemble learning technique that combines multiple weak predictive models to create a strong predictive model. It is a popular machine learning algorithm known for its high performance and ability to handle various types of data. Gradient Boosting works by iteratively training a sequence of patterns, where each subsequent pattern is built to correct the errors of previous patterns.

The algorithm begins by building an initial model, often a decision tree, which makes predictions about the target variable. The subsequent models are constructed to focus on cases where previous models have performed poorly. During each iteration, the algorithm assigns higher weights to misclassified instances and trains a new model to minimize errors. This iterative process continues until a specified number of models are trained or a desired level of performance is achieved.

The Concept of Boosting in Gradient Boosting

Boosting is a machine learning concept where multiple weak models are combined to create a powerful predictive model. In the context of Gradient Boosting, boosting refers to the process of sequentially adding weak learners (also known as Decision Trees) to the ensemble, with each subsequent learner focusing on correcting errors made by previous learners.

Weak learners refer to simple and relatively weak predictive models that are combined to create a strong overall model. These weak learners are often decision trees with limited depth or other simple models. The idea behind using weak learners is that even if they do not do well individually, their collective efforts and overall approach can lead to a powerful predictive model.

The boosting process begins with a weak initial learner, often referred to as the base learner. This base learner is trained on the dataset and predictions are made. The difference between the predicted values and the actual values is calculated, and this difference, also known as the residual error, becomes the target for the next weak learner.

Subsequent weak learners are then trained to predict the residual errors of previous learners. Each new learner focuses on minimizing the residual errors made by the ensemble up to that point. The predictions of all weak learners are then combined to produce the final ensemble prediction.

The boosting process continues iteratively, with each new weak learner attempting to improve the overall predictive performance of the ensemble. Through this iterative process, the ensemble progressively reduces the errors made by individual weak learners and produces a robust predictive model.

By combining predictions from multiple weak learners, Gradient Boosting is able to capture complex relationships in data and make accurate predictions. Boosting improves overall model performance and can be particularly effective in solving problems with high-dimensional or noisy data.

> **How to Identify if your problem can be solved using Gradient Boosting?**
>
> To determine if Gradient Boosting is appropriate for a specific problem, consider the characteristics of the problem and the available data. Gradient Boosting works well on numeric and categorical data and can handle large datasets with complex relationships. It is effective when the problem involves a trade-off between accuracy and interpretability. If the problem requires high predictive accuracy and the dataset contains informative features, Gradient Boosting may be an appropriate choice. Also, if the problem has a pattern of misclassifications or errors that can be fixed iteratively, Gradient Boosting can be an interesting approach.

Here is an implementation of Gradient Boosting on the breast cancer dataset from scikit-learn:

```python
from sklearn.datasets import load_breast_cancer
from sklearn.model_selection import train_test_split
from sklearn.ensemble import GradientBoostingClassifier
from sklearn.metrics import accuracy_score

# Load the breast cancer dataset
data = load_breast_cancer()
X, y = data.data, data.target

# Split the dataset into training and testing sets
X_train, X_test, y_train, y_test = train_test_split(X, y, test_size=0.2, random_state=42)

# Create a Gradient Boosting classifier
gb = GradientBoostingClassifier(n_estimators=100, learning_rate=0.1, random_state=42)
```

```python
# Train the classifier
gb.fit(X_train, y_train)

# Make predictions on the test set
y_pred = gb.predict(X_test)

# Evaluate the accuracy of the classifier
accuracy = accuracy_score(y_test, y_pred)
print("Accuracy:", accuracy)
```

Accuracy: 0.956140350877193

In the above implementation of the Gradient Boosting Classifier:

- n_estimators represents the number of weak learners that will be added sequentially to the ensemble. Increasing the number of estimators can improve model performance, but it can also lead to longer training time and increased complexity.

- learning_rate controls the contribution of each weak learner to the ensemble. It determines the amount of update of the weights of the misclassified samples at each iteration. A lower learning rate may result in a more conservative and accurate model, while a higher learning rate may lead to faster convergence but with a risk of overfitting.

Advantages & Disadvantages of Decision Trees and Ensemble Methods

Decision Trees offer several advantages in machine learning. They are easy to understand and interpret, as the tree structure represents a series of logical decisions. Decision Trees can handle both numerical and categorical data and are robust to missing values. They can be used for both classification and regression tasks. Ensemble Methods, such as Random Forests and Gradient Boosting, build upon the strengths of Decision Trees and provide additional benefits. Ensemble Methods can improve the accuracy and robustness of predictions by combining the predictions of multiple individual models. They can handle high-dimensional data and capture complex interactions between features.

However, Decision Trees and Ensemble Methods also have some limitations. Decision Trees are prone to overfitting and can create overly complex trees that may not generalize well to new data. Ensemble Methods, while effective, can be computationally expensive and require careful parameter tuning. Additionally, the interpretability of Ensemble Methods is reduced compared to individual Decision Trees. It's important to consider these advantages and disadvantages when choosing the appropriate algorithm for a specific Machine Learning problem.

Summary

In this chapter, we explored decision tree algorithms and ensemble methods, which are powerful Machine Learning techniques. We discovered various decision tree algorithms, including CART, ID3, and C4.5, which use different strategies to build decision trees based on the characteristics of the data. Additionally, we looked at Random Forests, an ensemble method that combines multiple decision trees to make more accurate predictions. We discussed the concept of bagging, which forms the basis of random forests, allowing individual trees to be trained on different subsets of data. Additionally, we explored Gradient Boosting, another ensemble method that builds patterns sequentially, with each pattern improving on the errors of previous ones. We discussed how boosting helps achieve high accuracy by iteratively refining model predictions.

Chapter 8: Boosting Algorithms

In the previous chapter, I introduced you to Decision trees and ensemble methods where we also discussed the concept of boosting. In this chapter, we will discuss the concept of boosting algorithms in detail.

Boosting Algorithms is a paradigm of Machine Learning where the amalgamation of weak learners gives rise to surprisingly powerful predictive models. Boosting is a testament to human ingenuity, ingeniously orchestrating collaboration and model cooperation to overcome the constraints of individual weak learners.

Boosting, in its purest form, represents a family of algorithms that iteratively improve the predictive ability of weak learners. These weak learners, although individually weak in their predictive abilities, are essential building blocks that collectively contribute to the creation of a robust ensemble model.

The concept of weak learners lies at the heart of boosting. These models exhibit modest predictive accuracy, often just marginally better than random guessing. However, despite their inherent limitations, weak learners possess a remarkable attribute—they can excel in different areas of the feature space. By identifying and leveraging this diversity, boosting algorithms amalgamate a multitude of weak learners, each specializing in a distinct facet of the problem at hand.

Boosting further elevates weak learners through a process of iterative learning. During each boosting iteration, the algorithm assigns higher weights to the instances that were previously misclassified or had high errors. By doing so, the boosting algorithm compels subsequent weak learners to focus on these challenging instances, thereby refining the ensemble's predictive abilities.

Moreover, boosting algorithms employ intelligent strategies to ensure that the ensemble as a whole surpasses the limitations of its components. Weaknesses of individual learners, such as high bias or overfitting, are mitigated through the iterative nature of boosting. By continually emphasizing the misclassified instances, boosting algorithms adaptively refine the ensemble, learning from past mistakes and steadily converging towards a more accurate model. Now, one may wonder how to identify whether the problem at hand is amenable to solving using boosting algorithms.

While not all problems are inherently suited for boosting, certain characteristics indicate the potential efficacy of this approach. Problems that exhibit heterogeneous or complex patterns, where no single model can capture the entire intricacy, often benefit from the collective intelligence of boosting. Additionally, domains where weak learners can be trained sequentially, capitalizing on the knowledge gained from previous iterations, are well-suited for boosting.

Throughout this chapter, we will explore boosting algorithms, their inner workings, and practical considerations for their application. By the end, you will possess the knowledge to discern when boosting algorithms can be leveraged to address your specific problem, opening doors to enhanced predictive capabilities and remarkable insights.

Getting Started with Adaboost

Adaboost, an abbreviated form of Adaptive Boosting, represents a remarkable achievement in machine learning, offering a powerful technique to elevate the predictive abilities of weak learners through a collaborative ensemble approach.

Adaboost is governed by a set of core principles that underpin its functionality and efficacy. By comprehending these principles, we can unravel the intricacies of Adaboost and grasp its unique qualities. Let us now delve into the essence of Adaboost and the core principles that shape its remarkable capabilities.

Adaboost, at its core, embraces the principle of iterative learning. It trains weak learners—models that possess modest predictive prowess—iteratively, improving their individual performance over time. This iterative approach allows Adaboost to refine the ensemble model progressively, fostering increased accuracy and reliability.

The second core principle of Adaboost lies in its emphasis on challenging instances. Adaboost assigns weights to the training instances, initially treating each instance as equally significant. However, as the iterations progress, Adaboost allocates higher weights to instances that were previously misclassified, highlighting their importance. By prioritizing the correct classification of these challenging instances, Adaboost directs subsequent weak learners to focus on these specific cases, augmenting the ensemble's ability to handle difficult situations.

An integral aspect of Adaboost is the formation of a weighted ensemble. As the iterations unfold, Adaboost assigns weights to the predictions made by each weak learner. The weight assigned to each weak learner's prediction is determined by its performance in the previous iterations. Consequently, the predictions of the more accurate weak learners hold greater weight in the final ensemble. Through this process, Adaboost blends the predictions of all weak learners, considering their individual expertise, to construct a robust ensemble model that excels in predictive accuracy.

The final core principle of Adaboost encompasses its adaptive nature. Adaboost learns from its past mistakes and adapts its learning process accordingly. By adjusting the weights of instances and prioritizing misclassified cases, Adaboost continuously refines the ensemble, leveraging the knowledge gained from previous iterations. This adaptability enables Adaboost to overcome the limitations of individual weak learners and evolve into a powerful predictive tool.

Together, these core principles—iterative learning, emphasizing challenging instances, weighted ensemble formation, and adaptability—contribute to the essence and effectiveness of Adaboost. By embracing these principles, Adaboost harnesses the collective intelligence of weak learners and transforms them into a force to be reckoned with.

The Boosting Process

In the captivating world of Adaboost lies a remarkable process that elevates the predictive capabilities of weak learners. This process, central to Adaboost, involves weight updates and error minimization, two pivotal steps that fuel the iterative refinement of the ensemble model.

Weight Updates:

The first step in the boosting process of Adaboost revolves around the concept of weight updates. At the outset, each training instance is assigned a weight, denoting its significance within the learning process. Initially, these weights are set uniformly, treating all instances as equally important.

As Adaboost progresses through its iterations, it adapts and adjusts these weights based on the performance of the weak learners. Instances that are misclassified or have higher errors in the previous iteration are assigned higher weights. By doing so, Adaboost bestows greater importance upon these challenging instances, urging subsequent weak learners to pay closer attention to them in the subsequent iterations.

This strategic adjustment of weights ensures that Adaboost places a heightened focus on those instances that present greater difficulty, enabling the ensemble model to improve its accuracy in handling complex and intricate patterns. The adaptability of Adaboost shines through its ability to allocate weights in a manner that reflects the evolving understanding of the data and the ensemble's learning trajectory.

Error Minimization:

The second vital aspect of the boosting process in Adaboost centres around error minimization. Once the weights are appropriately updated, Adaboost proceeds to train a weak learner on the modified training data. The aim is to minimize the errors made by the model during this iteration.

Through a meticulous learning process, the weak learner endeavours to capture the underlying patterns and relationships within the data, striving to make accurate predictions. However, the weak learner may still fall short of achieving perfect accuracy due to its inherent limitations.

After the weak learner completes their training, Adaboost assesses its performance by evaluating the errors it made on the weighted instances. The errors are quantified and serve as a measure of the weak learner's effectiveness in capturing the complexities of the data.

Adaboost leverages these error estimates to determine the significance of each weak learner's contribution to the ensemble. Weak learners with lower errors are given more weight in the subsequent ensemble construction, as they have demonstrated greater proficiency in understanding the data patterns. In contrast, weak learners with higher errors are assigned lesser weight, and their influence is correspondingly reduced.

By iteratively updating the weights of instances and minimizing errors through successive iterations, Adaboost assembles a powerful ensemble model that leverages the strengths of multiple weak learners. The iterative refinement of the ensemble, guided by weight updates and error minimization, imbues Adaboost with the ability to overcome the limitations of individual models and achieve enhanced predictive accuracy.

Implementation of AdaBoost

Here's how to implement the AdaBoost algorithm using Python:

```python
from sklearn.datasets import load_breast_cancer
from sklearn.ensemble import AdaBoostClassifier
from sklearn.tree import DecisionTreeClassifier
from sklearn.model_selection import train_test_split
from sklearn.metrics import accuracy_score

# Load the breast cancer dataset
data = load_breast_cancer()
X, y = data.data, data.target

X_train, X_test, y_train, y_test = train_test_split(X, y, test_size=0.2, random_state=42)

# Step 3: Instantiate the AdaBoost classifier
base_estimator = DecisionTreeClassifier(max_depth=1) # Decision stump as the weak learner
n_estimators = 100 # Number of iterations
learning_rate = 0.1 # Learning rate

adaBoost = AdaBoostClassifier(base_estimator=base_estimator, n_estimators=n_estimators, learning_rate=learning_rate)

# Step 4: Train the AdaBoost classifier
adaBoost.fit(X_train, y_train)
```

```python
# Step 5: Make predictions on unseen data
predictions = adaBoost.predict(X_test)

# Step 6: Evaluate the accuracy of the AdaBoost model
accuracy = accuracy_score(y_test, predictions)
print("Accuracy:", accuracy)
```

In this example, we import the necessary libraries including AdaBoostClassifier from sklearn.ensemble, DecisionTreeClassifier from sklearn.tree, train_test_split from sklearn.model_selection, and accuracy_score from sklearn.metrics.

After importing the data, we then split the data into training and testing subsets using train_test_split, where X represents the feature matrix and y represents the target variable.

Next, we instantiate the AdaBoost classifier with a decision stump (DecisionTreeClassifier(max_depth=1)) as the base estimator. We specify the number of iterations (n_estimators) and the learning rate (learning_rate), which control the algorithm's behaviour.

When applying AdaBoost in practice, several practical considerations come into play. Firstly, it is essential to carefully select weak learners, ensuring that they are appropriately suited to the problem at hand. Decision stumps, which are weak learners that make predictions based on a single feature, are commonly used in AdaBoost. However, other weak learners can also be employed, depending on the characteristics of the dataset.

Another crucial consideration is the size and representativeness of the training data. AdaBoost tends to perform better when trained on a sufficiently large and diverse dataset. Insufficient data or an imbalanced distribution of classes may hinder the algorithm's ability to generalize well. Thus, collecting a comprehensive and balanced training set is essential for optimal performance.

Furthermore, the hyperparameters of AdaBoost should be carefully tuned. The number of iterations (n_estimators) and the learning rate (learning_rate) influence the algorithm's performance and convergence.

Lastly, it is important to be mindful of the potential limitations of AdaBoost. It is susceptible to overfitting if the weak learners become too complex or if the number of iterations is excessively high. Regularization techniques, such as limiting the maximum depth of decision trees or reducing the learning rate, can help mitigate this risk.

XGBoost (Extreme Gradient Boosting)

XGBoost, short for Extreme Gradient Boosting, stands as a testament to the relentless pursuit of excellence and the relentless desire to push the boundaries of predictive modelling.

XGBoost has emerged as a prominent algorithm due to its exceptional performance, robustness, and versatility. It combines the principles of boosting with cutting-edge techniques to deliver outstanding predictive accuracy and handle diverse Machine Learning tasks.

XGBoost operates on the principles of boosting, seeking to iteratively improve weak learners and construct a robust ensemble model. At its core lies the concept of gradient boosting, where subsequent weak learners are trained to correct the errors made by previous learners. XGBoost amplifies this concept with its refined approach, leveraging the power of gradient information to enhance accuracy and efficiency.

XGBoost introduces an innovative technique known as gradient-based optimization, which enables it to handle diverse Machine Learning tasks effectively. It accomplishes this through the integration of a cost function that quantifies the difference between predicted and actual values. By calculating gradients from this cost function, XGBoost identifies the direction in which predictions need to be adjusted to minimize errors.

Furthermore, XGBoost employs an ensemble of decision trees as weak learners, with each tree capturing specific patterns in the data. These decision trees are constructed in a sequential manner, each learning from the errors of the previous tree to improve prediction accuracy. By combining the predictions of all trees in the ensemble, weighted according to their performance, XGBoost generates a powerful and comprehensive model.

Key Enhancements in XGBoost

XGBoost offers several key enhancements over traditional gradient boosting algorithms, empowering it with unparalleled capabilities. One significant enhancement lies in its regularization techniques, which combat overfitting and enhance generalization. XGBoost integrates L1 and L2 regularization, constraining the complexity of individual trees and controlling the magnitude of their parameters. This regularization ensures a balance between model flexibility and the avoidance of excessive complexity, leading to improved performance on unseen data.

Another notable enhancement in XGBoost is its ability to handle missing values gracefully. Real-world datasets often contain missing values, which can pose challenges for traditional algorithms. However, XGBoost implements a robust mechanism to handle missing data, ensuring that it can effectively learn from incomplete instances. By intelligently treating missing values as an additional category during tree construction, XGBoost enables accurate predictions even in the presence of missing data.

Parallelization is yet another powerful enhancement in XGBoost. By harnessing the capabilities of modern computing architectures, XGBoost can exploit parallel processing to accelerate training and prediction processes. This parallelization of computations significantly enhances the algorithm's scalability, enabling it to handle vast datasets and complex models more efficiently. As a result, XGBoost achieves exceptional speed and performance, even on large-scale problems.

Additionally, XGBoost incorporates advanced tree pruning techniques to optimize the structure of decision trees. By removing unnecessary branches, XGBoost reduces model complexity, prevents overfitting, and enhances interpretability. This strategic pruning strikes a delicate balance, allowing the model to capture important patterns while avoiding excessive memorization of the training data.

Implementation of XGBoost

Here's how to implement the XGBoost algorithm using Python:

```python
# Step 1: Import the necessary libraries
import xgboost as xgb
from sklearn.datasets import load_breast_cancer
from sklearn.model_selection import train_test_split
from sklearn.metrics import accuracy_score

# Load the breast cancer dataset
data = load_breast_cancer()
X, y = data.data, data.target

X_train, X_test, y_train, y_test = train_test_split(X, y, test_size=0.2, random_state=42)

# Step 3: Instantiate the XGBoost classifier
xgb_model = xgb.XGBClassifier(n_estimators=100, learning_rate=0.1)

# Step 4: Train the XGBoost classifier
xgb_model.fit(X_train, y_train)

# Step 5: Make predictions on unseen data
```

```python
predictions = xgb_model.predict(X_test)

# Step 6: Evaluate the accuracy of the XGBoost model
accuracy = accuracy_score(y_test, predictions)
print("Accuracy:", accuracy)
```

Accuracy: 0.9649122807017544

When applying XGBoost in practice, several practical considerations come into play. It is crucial to carefully select appropriate hyperparameters based on the characteristics of the dataset and the specific requirements of the problem at hand. Tuning hyperparameters, such as the learning rate, number of boosting rounds, and maximum depth of trees, can significantly impact the model's performance.

Feature engineering, including data preprocessing, handling categorical variables, and dealing with missing values, is another critical aspect. Properly preparing the data can enhance the effectiveness of XGBoost and improve its predictive accuracy.

Furthermore, XGBoost provides various options for parallelization and distributed computing, which can greatly speed up the training process, particularly for large datasets. Utilizing these features effectively can expedite model development and deployment.

Summary

So Boosting algorithms, such as Adaboost and XGBoost, are remarkable techniques in the field of machine learning that aim to improve predictive accuracy by combining the strengths of multiple weak learners. Adaboost, with its core principles of iterative learning and emphasizing challenging instances, adapts to progressively refine the ensemble model. XGBoost, an evolution of traditional gradient boosting, introduces regularization techniques, graceful handling of missing values, and advanced tree pruning to enhance model performance. With its remarkable advancements, XGBoost has gained recognition for its exceptional predictive accuracy, robustness, and versatility. These boosting algorithms, including Adaboost and XGBoost, stand as a testament to the relentless pursuit of excellence in the field of machine learning, empowering practitioners to tackle complex predictive modelling tasks with confidence.

Chapter 9: Clustering Algorithms

In this chapter, we will dive deep into clustering algorithms in Machine Learning. Clustering algorithms aim to identify patterns and group similar data points together. Clustering algorithms possess the ability to uncover inherent structures and relationships within unlabeled datasets, allowing for the extraction of meaningful insights. These algorithms are particularly useful when working with large and complex datasets, where manual examination and categorization become arduous or even infeasible tasks. By employing various mathematical techniques, clustering algorithms offer a systematic approach to organizing and partitioning data, enabling researchers and practitioners to discern coherent clusters and gain valuable knowledge about the underlying dataset.

Clustering algorithms find their utility across a wide range of applications and industries. Whenever there is a need to uncover hidden structures or group similar data points together, clustering algorithms become invaluable tools. Some common scenarios where clustering algorithms are applicable include:

- Customer Segmentation: Clustering algorithms aid businesses in segmenting their customer base based on purchasing behaviour, demographics, or other relevant attributes. This segmentation can facilitate targeted marketing strategies and personalized services, leading to improved customer satisfaction and increased sales.

- Image and Document Classification: Clustering algorithms can assist in organizing and categorizing large collections of images or documents. By automatically identifying similar images or documents, clustering algorithms simplify the task of information retrieval and content organization.

- Anomaly Detection: Clustering algorithms can be employed to identify anomalies or outliers within a dataset. By distinguishing unusual patterns or observations, clustering algorithms contribute to fraud detection, network intrusion detection, and other anomaly detection tasks.

- Biological Data Analysis: Clustering algorithms are extensively used in bioinformatics and genomics to identify clusters of genes or proteins with similar expression patterns. These clusters can provide valuable insights into disease classification, drug discovery, and biological processes.

- Social Network Analysis: Clustering algorithms can be employed to analyze social networks and identify communities or groups of individuals with similar interests or connections. This information can assist in targeted advertising, recommendation systems, and understanding social dynamics.

Clustering algorithms encompass a diverse array of methods, each designed to address specific data characteristics and objectives. The following are some commonly used types of clustering algorithms:

- K-Means Clustering: K-Means clustering is a method that aims to partition a dataset into a specified number of distinct clusters. It accomplishes this by iteratively assigning data points to the cluster whose mean is closest to them and then recalculating the mean of each cluster. This process continues until the clusters stabilize and no further changes occur. K-Means clustering is based on the principle of minimizing the total intra-cluster variance, seeking to form clusters with minimal internal distance and maximal separation between clusters.

- DBSCAN Clustering: DBSCAN (Density-Based Spatial Clustering of Applications with Noise) is a clustering algorithm that groups together data points based on their density in the data space. It defines clusters as regions of high density, separated by regions of low density. DBSCAN identifies core points that have a sufficient number of neighbouring points within a specified distance and expands clusters around these core points. It also detects outliers or noise points that lie in regions of low density and do not belong to any cluster. DBSCAN is capable of discovering clusters of arbitrary shape and size.

- Agglomerative Clustering: Agglomerative clustering is a hierarchical clustering algorithm that begins by treating each data point as an individual cluster. It then merges the closest pairs of clusters at each step, gradually building a tree-like structure known as a dendrogram. The merging process continues until all data points belong to a single cluster. Agglomerative clustering can be based on different distance metrics, such as Euclidean distance or Manhattan distance, and uses linkage criteria (e.g., single linkage, complete linkage, or average linkage) to determine the distance between clusters during the merging process.

- BIRCH Clustering: BIRCH (Balanced Iterative Reducing and Clustering using Hierarchies) clustering is a hierarchical clustering algorithm designed for large datasets. It constructs a hierarchical structure by incrementally clustering data points into subclusters. BIRCH uses a compact and efficient data structure called the Clustering Feature Tree (CFT) to summarize the distribution of data within subclusters. The algorithm iteratively merges the subclusters, reducing the number of subclusters and forming a hierarchy. BIRCH can handle large datasets efficiently by minimizing I/O operations and memory requirements.

- Mean-Shift Clustering: Mean-Shift clustering is a non-parametric algorithm that seeks to identify clusters by finding high-density regions in the data space. It starts by placing a window or kernel at each data point and iteratively shifts the centre of the window towards regions of higher density, guided by the mean shift vector. The mean shift vector is calculated as the weighted average of the data points within the window. The algorithm converges when the window centres no longer move. Mean-Shift clustering is capable of identifying clusters of various shapes and sizes and does not require specifying the number of clusters in advance.

In the rest of the chapter, we will explore all these clustering algorithms one by one.

K-means

The K-means algorithm is a popular unsupervised Machine Learning technique used for clustering data points into groups. It aims to find the K number of clusters in the data, where K is a pre-defined value. Each cluster represents a group of data points that are similar to each other, while data points in different clusters are dissimilar. K-means is an iterative algorithm that minimizes the sum of squared distances between data points and their respective cluster centroids.

The K-means algorithm starts by randomly selecting K data points as initial centroids. These centroids serve as the centre points for the clusters. Then, each data point is assigned to the nearest centroid based on their Euclidean distance, forming the initial clusters.

After the assignment, the algorithm recalculates the centroid of each cluster by taking the mean of all the data points assigned to that cluster. These updated centroids become the new centre points. This process of assignment and updating is repeated iteratively until convergence is achieved. Convergence happens when the centroids no longer change significantly or when a maximum number of iterations is reached.

Once the algorithm converges, the data points are classified into K clusters based on the final centroids, representing the final clustering outcome.

To assess if K-means is appropriate, it is helpful to examine the nature of the data and the problem's requirements. Consider whether the problem involves numeric data or features that can be quantified and compared using distance measures. K-means is primarily designed for numerical data, where the Euclidean distance metric is commonly used. Additionally, K-means assumes that each data point can be assigned to only one cluster, known as hard clustering.

Another consideration is the desired output. K-means aims to partition the data into a fixed number of clusters, which need to be predefined. If the problem requires a different type of output, such as hierarchical clustering or density-based clustering, alternative algorithms may be more suitable.

Furthermore, it is important to evaluate the underlying assumptions of K-means for the specific problem. The algorithm assumes that the clusters have similar variances and densities, and the clusters are spherical and have equal sizes. If these assumptions do not align with the problem's characteristics, it may impact the effectiveness of K-means.

Implementation of K-means

Several practical considerations should be taken into account when implementing the K-means algorithm. Firstly, selecting an appropriate value for K is crucial and can be based on domain knowledge or techniques like the elbow method or silhouette analysis.

The initialization of centroids is also important, as different strategies such as random selection or k-means initialization can impact convergence and cluster quality. Setting a maximum number of iterations is necessary to avoid infinite running, typically stopping when centroids no longer change significantly.

Preprocessing the data by scaling or normalizing features ensures equal importance across dimensions. Handling outliers, which can significantly affect results, may require separate treatment or removal from the dataset.

Here's how to implement the K-means algorithm using Python:

```python
from sklearn.cluster import KMeans
from sklearn.datasets import make_blobs

# Generating synthetic data for clustering
X, _ = make_blobs(n_samples=100, centers=3, random_state=42)

# Creating an instance of KMeans algorithm
kmeans = KMeans(n_clusters=3, init='random', random_state=42)

# Fitting the algorithm to the data
kmeans.fit(X)

# Obtaining the cluster labels for each data point
labels = kmeans.labels_
```

In this implementation, we start by importing the necessary modules: KMeans from sklearn.cluster for the K-means algorithm and make_blobs from sklearn.datasets to generate synthetic data for clustering.

Next, we generate a synthetic dataset using make_blobs. This dataset contains 100 samples distributed across 3 clusters. The data is stored in the variable X, while the target labels (which are not used in unsupervised learning) are discarded with _.

Then, we create an instance of the KMeans algorithm by calling KMeans(). We specify the number of clusters n_clusters as 3, representing the desired number of clusters in the data. The init parameter determines the method for initializing the centroids, and in this case, we use 'random' initialization. The random_state parameter ensures the reproducibility of the results.

After creating the KMeans object, we fit the algorithm to the data by calling kmeans.fit(X). This step performs the actual clustering, where the algorithm iteratively assigns data points to the nearest centroid and updates the centroid positions until convergence.

Once the algorithm has converged, we can obtain the cluster labels for each data point by accessing kmeans.labels_. These labels indicate which cluster each data point belongs to.

Here's how to visualize the clusters:

```python
import plotly.express as px
import pandas as pd
# Creating a DataFrame with the data and cluster labels
df = pd.DataFrame(X, columns=['x', 'y'])
df['cluster'] = labels.astype(str)

# Visualizing the clusters
fig = px.scatter(df, x='x', y='y', color='cluster', title='K-means Clustering')
fig.show()
```

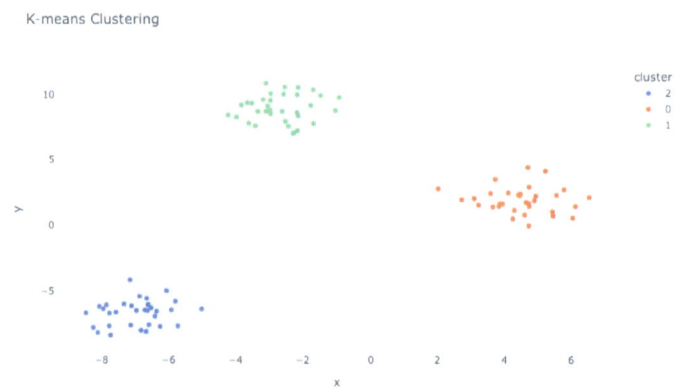

Advantages & Disadvantages of K-means

The K-means algorithm has several advantages. Firstly, it is computationally efficient and scalable, making it suitable for large datasets. Additionally, it is easy to understand and implement, requiring minimal parameter tuning. K-means can handle a variety of data types and is particularly effective for well-separated, spherical clusters. It is also widely used in practice and has been extensively studied and validated in various applications.

However, K-means has certain limitations. It requires the user to specify the number of clusters, which can be challenging in real-world scenarios. The algorithm is sensitive to the initial centroid placement, leading to different outcomes for different initializations. K-means assumes that clusters have similar sizes and variances, which may not hold true in all datasets. Furthermore, it can be influenced by outliers and noise, affecting the clustering results. Overall, while K-means offers simplicity and efficiency, its performance may vary depending on the dataset characteristics and appropriate considerations must be taken into account during its application.

DBSCAN

DBSCAN (Density-Based Spatial Clustering of Applications with Noise) is a popular algorithm used for clustering data points based on their spatial density. It is particularly effective when dealing with datasets that contain irregularly shaped clusters and noise.

The DBSCAN algorithm operates by defining clusters based on two main parameters: the radius of a neighbourhood around each data point and the minimum number of data points required within that radius to form a dense region. These parameters allow DBSCAN to identify core points, border points, and noise points within the dataset.

DBSCAN works by randomly selecting a data point that has not been assigned to a cluster. If this point has a sufficient number of neighbouring points within its defined radius, a new cluster is created. The algorithm then expands the cluster by iteratively adding more neighbouring points to it, ultimately capturing all density-reachable points within the neighbourhood. The process continues until no more data points can be added to the cluster. At this point, the algorithm selects a new unassigned point and repeats the process to find another cluster or noise point. The algorithm terminates when all data points have been assigned to clusters or marked as noise.

Determining whether a problem can be effectively solved using DBSCAN depends on the nature of the data and the desired outcome. DBSCAN is suitable for datasets with varying cluster shapes, as it can identify clusters of different densities and handle noise points. It is particularly useful when prior knowledge about the number of clusters is unavailable or when dealing with complex, high-dimensional datasets.

Implementation of DBSCAN

Practical considerations when implementing DBSCAN include determining the appropriate values for the radius and the minimum number of points required within the radius. These parameters heavily influence the clustering outcome, and selecting them correctly is crucial. In some cases, trial and error or domain knowledge may be required to find optimal values.

Here's how to implement the DBSCAN algorithm using Python:

```python
from sklearn.cluster import DBSCAN
from sklearn.datasets import make_blobs

# Generating synthetic data for clustering
X, _ = make_blobs(n_samples=100, centers=3, random_state=42)

# Creating an instance of the DBSCAN class
dbscan = DBSCAN(eps=0.5, min_samples=5)

# Fitting the DBSCAN model to the data
dbscan.fit(X)

# Accessing the labels assigned to each data point
labels = dbscan.labels_
```

DBSCAN clustering has two main parameters:

- eps (epsilon): This parameter determines the radius of the neighbourhood around each data point. It specifies the maximum distance between two points for them to be considered neighbours. Smaller values of eps result in tighter, more dense clusters, while larger values allow for more expansive clusters.

- min_samples: This parameter specifies the minimum number of data points required within the eps radius to form a dense region or core point. Points that do not meet this requirement are considered noise. Larger values of min_samples lead to more conservative clustering, requiring a higher density of points to form clusters.

Here's how to visualize the clusters:

```
df = pd.DataFrame(X, columns=['x', 'y'])
df['cluster'] = labels.astype(str)

# Visualizing the clusters
fig = px.scatter(df, x='x', y='y', color='cluster', title='DBSCAN Clustering')
fig.show()
```

We can see that some of the clusters are overlapping here. This situation arises because DBSCAN allows for clusters of different densities and irregular shapes. It identifies clusters based on the density of data points in their local neighbourhoods. Therefore, it is possible to have overlapping or adjacent clusters if there is a gradual transition or density variation between them.

Advantages & Disadvantages of DBSCAN

DBSCAN has several advantages that make it a popular clustering algorithm. Firstly, it can discover clusters of arbitrary shape and size, making it effective for datasets with irregular cluster geometries. DBSCAN also handles noise and outlier detection well, as it identifies them as individual points not belonging to any cluster. Moreover, DBSCAN does not require specifying the number of clusters in advance, which is beneficial when prior knowledge about the data is limited.

However, DBSCAN has a few limitations. It struggles with datasets where clusters have significantly different densities or when clusters overlap extensively. Selecting appropriate parameter values, such as the radius and minimum number of points, can be challenging and sensitive to the dataset. Additionally, DBSCAN's computational complexity increases with larger datasets, making it less efficient for very large datasets.

Agglomerative Clustering

Agglomerative Clustering is a hierarchical clustering algorithm used in machine learning to group similar data points together. It operates by iteratively merging the most similar pairs of data points until a desired number of clusters is achieved.

The algorithm begins by assigning each data point to its own cluster. Then, it calculates the similarity or dissimilarity between pairs of clusters using a distance metric, such as Euclidean distance or cosine similarity. The two clusters with the smallest distance are merged into a single cluster. This process is repeated until all data points belong to a single cluster or the desired number of clusters is reached.

The similarity or dissimilarity between clusters can be calculated in different ways, such as single linkage, complete linkage, or average linkage. In a single linkage, the distance between two clusters is determined by the shortest distance between any two points from the two clusters. In complete linkage, the distance is determined by the longest distance between any two points. Average linkage considers the average distance between all pairs of points from the two clusters.

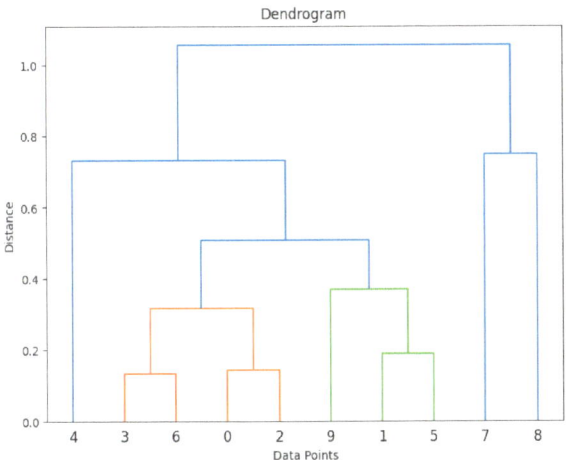

During the merging process, a hierarchical structure is formed, where clusters are nested within larger clusters. This structure can be represented using a dendrogram, which is a tree-like diagram that illustrates the merging process, as shown in the image.

Determining if Agglomerative Clustering is suitable for a specific problem depends on the nature of the data and the objectives of the analysis. Agglomerative Clustering is particularly useful when dealing with hierarchical or nested structures in the data, where the formation of clusters at different levels of granularity is desired. It is also effective when the number of clusters is unknown or needs to be determined based on the data.

However, Agglomerative Clustering may not be suitable for datasets with high dimensionality or when dealing with large datasets due to computational limitations. Additionally, if the data does not exhibit any hierarchical or nested patterns, alternative clustering algorithms may be more appropriate.

Implementation of Agglomerative Clustering

When implementing Agglomerative Clustering, there are practical considerations to keep in mind. One important aspect is the choice of distance metric and linkage criterion, as they can significantly impact the clustering results. It is essential to select appropriate metrics based on the characteristics of the data and the desired clustering outcome.

Another consideration is the computational complexity of the algorithm. Agglomerative Clustering can be computationally expensive, especially for large datasets, as it requires calculating pairwise distances between clusters at each iteration. Therefore, it is crucial to optimize the implementation and consider alternative algorithms for scalability.

Here's how to implement the Agglomerative clustering algorithm using Python:

```
from sklearn.cluster import AgglomerativeClustering
from sklearn.datasets import make_blobs

# Generating synthetic data for clustering
X, _ = make_blobs(n_samples=100, random_state=42)

# Perform Agglomerative Clustering
agglomerative = AgglomerativeClustering(n_clusters=3)
labels = agglomerative.fit_predict(X)
```

We created an instance of AgglomerativeClustering and specified the number of clusters we want to identify using the n_clusters parameter. In this example, we set n_clusters to 3. Other optional parameters include the linkage parameter, which determines the linkage criterion used to calculate the distance between clusters (default is "ward"), and the affinity parameter, which specifies the distance metric to be used (default is "euclidean").

Here's how to visualize the clusters:

```python
import pandas as pd
import plotly.express as px

df = pd.DataFrame(X, columns=['x', 'y'])
df['cluster'] = labels.astype(str)

# Visualizing the clusters
fig = px.scatter(df, x='x', y='y', color='cluster', title='Agglomerative Clustering')
fig.show()
```

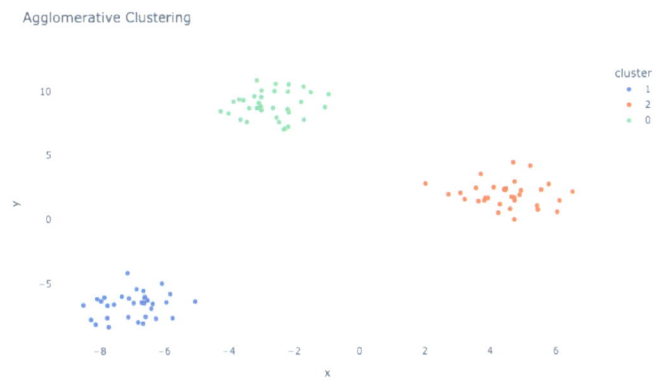

Advantages & Disadvantages of Agglomerative Clustering

Agglomerative Clustering has several advantages and disadvantages. On the positive side, one major advantage is its ability to discover hierarchical structures within the data. By iteratively merging clusters,

Agglomerative Clustering forms a hierarchy of clusters, allowing for a comprehensive understanding of the relationships and nested patterns present in the data. Additionally, Agglomerative Clustering does not require the number of clusters to be predefined, making it suitable for situations where the optimal number of clusters is unknown.

However, Agglomerative Clustering has some drawbacks. It can be computationally expensive, especially for large datasets, due to the need to calculate pairwise distances between clusters at each iteration. Additionally, the algorithm may struggle with high-dimensional data, as the distance calculations become less reliable in higher dimensions. Moreover, Agglomerative Clustering assumes that the clusters have a spherical shape and similar variances, which can limit its effectiveness for datasets with complex shapes or varying variances.

BIRCH Clustering

BIRCH (Balanced Iterative Reducing and Clustering using Hierarchies) is a clustering algorithm in Machine Learning that aims to efficiently cluster large amounts of data by constructing a hierarchical representation of the data. It was developed to handle high-dimensional and large-scale datasets.

The BIRCH Clustering algorithm works by iteratively reducing and clustering the data in a hierarchical manner. It starts by constructing a compact summary of the data called the Clustering Feature (CF) tree. The CF tree is a hierarchical structure that represents the distribution of data points in each cluster. It consists of three types of nodes: the entry node, the non-leaf nodes, and the leaf nodes.

Initially, the algorithm scans the input data and builds the CF tree incrementally. It employs a clustering criterion called the Branching

Factor (BF) to determine when to create a new node or merge existing nodes in the tree. The BF specifies the maximum number of children a node can have before it is split into two or more nodes. By dynamically adjusting the BF during the construction of the tree, BIRCH can adapt to the distribution of the data and form clusters of varying shapes and sizes.

Once the CF tree is constructed, the algorithm performs a global clustering step called Cluster-Feature (CF) clustering. This step further refines the clustering by merging similar clusters based on a distance measure. The CF clustering is based on the CF tree's structure and the thresholds defined for merging clusters. The final result is a set of clusters, each represented by its centroid and the number of points it contains.

To determine if the problem at hand can be solved using BIRCH Clustering, several factors should be considered. First, BIRCH is suitable for datasets with a large number of instances and high dimensionality, whereas other traditional clustering algorithms may struggle due to computational limitations. Second, the nature of the problem should involve the identification of natural clusters within the data. BIRCH assumes that the data points within a cluster have similar characteristics, and it aims to group them accordingly. Finally, BIRCH is most effective when the clusters are well separated, meaning there is a clear distinction between different groups of data points.

Implementation of BIRCH Clustering

When implementing BIRCH Clustering, there are practical considerations to keep in mind. One important aspect is the choice of distance measure, as it influences the accuracy and performance of the algorithm. Common distance measures used in BIRCH include

Euclidean distance for numerical data and cosine similarity for text data.

Additionally, the selection of parameters such as the branching factor and thresholds for merging clusters should be carefully tuned based on the characteristics of the dataset. Efficient data structures, such as balanced trees or hash tables, can also be employed to speed up the algorithm's computations.

Lastly, preprocessing steps like data normalization or dimensionality reduction techniques can be applied to enhance the clustering results and reduce the computational complexity.

Here's how to implement the BIRCH clustering algorithm using Python:

```python
from sklearn.cluster import Birch
from sklearn.datasets import make_blobs

# Generating synthetic data for clustering
X, _ = make_blobs(n_samples=100, random_state=42)

# BIRCH Clustering
birch = Birch(threshold=0.5, branching_factor=50)
birch.fit(X)

# Obtaining cluster labels
labels = birch.labels_
```

We created an instance of the Birch class with certain parameters. The threshold parameter determines the maximum radius of a subcluster and influences the final clustering structure. The branching_factor parameter sets the maximum number of children that a non-leaf node can have before it is split into multiple nodes.

Here's how to visualize the clusters:

```python
df = pd.DataFrame(X, columns=['x', 'y'])
df['cluster'] = labels.astype(str)

# Visualizing the clusters
```

```
fig = px.scatter(df, x='x', y='y', color='cluster', title='BIRCH Clustering')
fig.show()
```

The BIRCH algorithm automatically identifies the clusters in the data based on the defined parameters.

Advantages & Disadvantages of BIRCH Clustering

BIRCH clustering offers several advantages. Firstly, it is efficient in handling large-scale datasets as it constructs a compact summary of the data using the CF tree structure, reducing the computational complexity compared to other clustering algorithms. Secondly, BIRCH is capable of handling high-dimensional data, making it suitable for applications with a large number of features. Additionally, BIRCH is able to adapt to varying cluster shapes and sizes by dynamically adjusting the branching factor during tree construction.

However, BIRCH clustering also has certain limitations. It is sensitive to the choice of parameters such as the threshold and branching factor, which require careful tuning for optimal results. Furthermore,

BIRCH may struggle with datasets where clusters have complex and overlapping structures, as it assumes well-separated clusters. Overall, while BIRCH offers efficiency and scalability advantages, its performance can be affected by parameter selection and the nature of the dataset.

Mean Shift Clustering

Mean Shift Clustering is a Machine Learning algorithm used for clustering, which aims to group data points based on their similarity. It is a non-parametric algorithm, meaning it does not assume any particular distribution for the data. The goal of Mean Shift Clustering is to discover the underlying structure or patterns in the data without prior knowledge of the number of clusters.

The Mean Shift Clustering algorithm starts by randomly assigning each data point as a centroid or a representative point. It then iteratively shifts each point towards the higher-density regions of the data. This shifting process is guided by a kernel function, which determines the weight given to each neighbouring point.

At each iteration, the algorithm calculates the mean shift vector for each point by finding the weighted average of the vectors pointing towards the neighbouring points. The weights are determined by the kernel function, which assigns higher weights to points closer to the centre point. The mean shift vector represents the direction towards the higher-density regions of the data.

The algorithm continues shifting each point until convergence, which occurs when the mean shift vectors become small or negligible. At this point, the algorithm assigns each point to the cluster associated with the nearest converged centroid.

Mean Shift Clustering is suitable for problems where the underlying data distribution is unknown or when the number of clusters is not predetermined. It works well for data with irregular shapes and varying densities. It can be applied to various domains such as image segmentation, object tracking, and customer segmentation in marketing.

To determine if Mean Shift Clustering is appropriate for a problem, it is important to consider the nature of the data and the desired outcome. If there is a need to discover natural groupings or patterns in the data without prior assumptions about the number of clusters, Mean Shift Clustering can be a suitable choice.

Implementation of Mean Shift Clustering

When implementing Mean Shift Clustering, there are several practical considerations to keep in mind. Here are a few important ones:

- The choice of bandwidth parameter for the kernel function plays a crucial role in the algorithm's performance. It determines the size of the region used to calculate the mean shift vector. An appropriate bandwidth should be selected to capture the desired level of clustering granularity.

- Mean Shift Clustering can be computationally intensive, especially for large datasets. Various techniques such as kernel density estimation approximation and spatial data structures can be employed to improve efficiency.

- Defining the convergence criteria is important to determine when the algorithm should stop iterating. Typically, the mean shift vectors' magnitude or the number of iterations can be used as convergence criteria.

- Mean Shift Clustering may encounter challenges with scalability when dealing with high-dimensional data. Preprocessing techniques like dimensionality reduction can be applied to address this issue.

Here's how to implement the Mean Shift clustering algorithm using Python:

```python
from sklearn.cluster import MeanShift
from sklearn.datasets import make_blobs

# Generating synthetic data for clustering
X, _ = make_blobs(n_samples=100, random_state=42)

# Applying Mean Shift Clustering
ms = MeanShift()
ms.fit(X)

# Obtaining the cluster labels
labels = ms.labels_
```

The Mean Shift algorithm does not have many configurable parameters. However, it does have a bandwidth parameter that determines the size of the region used to calculate the mean shift vector. By default, this parameter is estimated automatically based on the data. Additionally, the algorithm has a bin_seeding parameter, which determines whether initial cluster centres should be set using a binning process. If set to True, it can help improve algorithm efficiency.

Advantages & Disadvantages of Mean Shift Clustering

Mean Shift clustering, similar to other clustering algorithms, possesses its own advantages and disadvantages. One advantage of Mean Shift clustering is its ability to discover clusters with arbitrary shapes and varying densities, making it suitable for datasets that do not adhere to traditional cluster assumptions. It does not require prior knowledge of the number of clusters, as it dynamically determines the number based on the data. Moreover, Mean Shift clustering can handle outliers effectively by shifting them towards the nearest cluster.

However, a disadvantage of Mean Shift clustering is its computationally intensive nature, especially for large datasets. The algorithm's performance heavily depends on the bandwidth parameter selection, which determines the size of the region used for shifting. Additionally, Mean Shift clustering struggles with high-dimensional data due to the curse of dimensionality. Preprocessing techniques like dimensionality reduction may be necessary to alleviate this issue.

Summary

In this chapter, we explored Clustering algorithms. Clustering algorithms encompass a diverse array of methods, each designed to address specific data characteristics and objectives. The following are some commonly used types of clustering algorithms that we explored in this chapter:

- K-Means Clustering: K-Means clustering is a method that aims to partition a dataset into a specified number of distinct clusters. It accomplishes this by iteratively assigning data points to the cluster whose mean is closest to them and then recalculating the mean of each cluster. This process continues until the clusters stabilize and no further changes occur. K-Means clustering is based on the principle of minimizing the total intra-cluster variance, seeking to form clusters with minimal internal distance and maximal separation between clusters.

- DBSCAN Clustering: DBSCAN (Density-Based Spatial Clustering of Applications with Noise) is a clustering algorithm that groups together data points based on their density in the data space. It defines clusters as regions of high density, separated by regions of low density. DBSCAN identifies core points that have a sufficient number of neighbouring points within a specified distance and expands clusters around these core points. It also detects outliers or noise points that lie in regions of low density and do not belong to any cluster. DBSCAN is capable of discovering clusters of arbitrary shape and size.

- Agglomerative Clustering: Agglomerative clustering is a hierarchical clustering algorithm that begins by treating each data point as an individual cluster. It then merges the closest pairs of clusters at each step, gradually building a tree-like structure known as a dendrogram. The merging process continues until all data points belong to a single cluster. Agglomerative clustering can be based on different distance metrics, such as Euclidean distance or Manhattan distance, and uses linkage criteria (e.g., single linkage, complete linkage, or average linkage) to determine the distance between clusters during the merging process.

- BIRCH Clustering: BIRCH (Balanced Iterative Reducing and Clustering using Hierarchies) clustering is a hierarchical clustering algorithm designed for large datasets. It constructs a hierarchical structure by incrementally clustering data points into subclusters. BIRCH uses a compact and efficient data structure called the Clustering Feature Tree (CFT) to summarize the distribution of data within subclusters. The algorithm iteratively merges the subclusters, reducing the number of subclusters and forming a hierarchy. BIRCH can handle large datasets efficiently by minimizing I/O operations and memory requirements.

- Mean-Shift Clustering: Mean-Shift clustering is a non-parametric algorithm that seeks to identify clusters by finding high-density regions in the data space. It starts by placing a window or kernel at each data point and iteratively shifts the centre of the window towards regions of higher density, guided by the mean shift vector. The mean shift vector is calculated as the weighted average of the data points within the window. The algorithm converges when the window centres no longer move. Mean-Shift clustering is capable of identifying clusters of various shapes and sizes and does not require specifying the number of clusters in advance.

Chapter 10: Important Data Preprocessing Elements To Train Better Models

In this chapter, we will uncover the important techniques for preparing data before training a model. Data often comes in a messy form, so we need to clean it up by handling missing information and dealing with outliers. We will also learn how to select the most relevant features in our data and scale them properly, so our models can understand them better.

Next, we will dive into model optimization techniques. Models have certain settings called hyperparameters that we can adjust to improve their performance. We will explore different methods to find the best hyperparameter settings, such as trying out different combinations systematically or using more advanced approaches. Sampling techniques are another important aspect we will explore. We will learn about resampling techniques that help us handle imbalanced data where some classes are underrepresented.

By understanding and applying these important elements, we will equip ourselves with the tools and knowledge to train better machine learning models.

Getting Started with Handling Missing Values

Missing values are the absence or nonexistence of particular observations or measurements within a dataset. These vacant slots in the dataset indicate the lack of information or data points for specific variables or entities under examination. The presence of missing values can arise due to a variety of factors, such as errors in data collection processes, respondents' non-responsiveness, or technical malfunctions during data recording.

One of the techniques to handle missing values is known as imputation, which entails estimating or filling in the missing values using relevant statistical techniques. Imputation seeks to replace the absent values with plausible substitutes based on the available data. Several imputation techniques exist, each with its own strengths and limitations, offering analysts the flexibility to choose the most suitable method for their specific dataset.

One common imputation technique involves the use of central tendency measures, such as the mean, median, or mode, to substitute missing values. By calculating the average or most frequent value within a variable, analysts can fill in the gaps with reasonable estimations that align with the overall distribution of the data. This technique assumes that the missing values are similar to the observed values within the same variable.

Here's an example of how to use measures of central tendency in filling missing values in a dataset using Python:

```python
import pandas as pd
import numpy as np

# creating a sample data
data = pd.DataFrame({'Height': [160, 170, np.nan, 180, 175, np.nan, 165, 172, 168]})

# calculating mean, median, and mode of the height feature
mean_height = data['Height'].mean()
median_height = data['Height'].median()
mode_height = data['Height'].mode().values[0]

# using mean height to fill missing values
data['Height'].fillna(mean_height, inplace=True)
```

In this example, we fill the missing values with the mean height.

The choice of the measure of central tendency depends on the nature of the data and the specific requirements of the analysis. When deciding whether to use the mean, median, or mode to fill in missing values in a dataset, it's important to consider the characteristics of the data and the specific requirements of the analysis. Here are some guidelines on when to prefer each measure:

- The mean is the most commonly used measure of central tendency. It represents the average value of the dataset and is suitable when the data is approximately normally distributed without significant outliers. The mean is influenced by extreme values, so if your dataset has outliers that could distort the average, it might be better to consider the median instead.

- The median is the middle value in a dataset when it is sorted in ascending or descending order. It is less affected by extreme values or outliers compared to the mean. The median is preferred when the data has outliers or when the distribution is skewed, as it provides a more robust estimate of the central tendency.

- The mode represents the most frequently occurring value in a dataset. It is useful for categorical or discrete data, where finding the most common category or value is meaningful. The mode can also be used for numerical data, but it may not provide a comprehensive summary of the dataset if there is no clear mode or when multiple values have similar frequencies.

Handling Outliers

Outliers are data points that deviate significantly from the rest of the data. These data points lie far away from the majority of the observations and can have a substantial impact on statistical analyses and modelling. Outliers can be caused by various factors such as measurement errors, data entry mistakes, or rare occurrences in the underlying phenomenon being studied. Identifying and handling outliers is crucial for maintaining the integrity and accuracy of data analysis.

Detecting outliers involves the process of identifying data points that appear to be unusually distant from the bulk of the data distribution. There are several statistical methods to detect outliers, including:

- Z-Score Method: This method measures how many standard deviations a data point is away from the mean. Data points with a Z-score greater than a predefined threshold (often 2 or 3) are considered outliers.

- IQR (Interquartile Range) Method: The IQR is the range between the 75th and 25th percentiles of the data. Data points lying below Q1 - 1.5 * IQR or above Q3 + 1.5 * IQR are considered outliers.

- Visualization: Plotting the data on a box plot or scatter plot can help visually identify outliers that fall far outside the main cluster of data points.

After detecting outliers, one can choose to handle them in different ways. Common approaches include:

- Removing Outliers: Simply excluding the identified outliers from the dataset can be an option, especially if they are caused by data entry errors or have a negligible impact on the overall analysis.

- Transforming Data: Applying data transformations, such as logarithmic or square root transformations, can mitigate the effect of outliers.

- Imputation: Replacing outliers with more reasonable values can be done through imputation techniques like using the median or mean of the non-outlying data points.

Let's create a sample dataset with outliers and detect and remove them using Python:

```python
import numpy as np
import pandas as pd

# Create a sample dataset with outliers
np.random.seed(42)
data = pd.DataFrame({
'Feature_A': np.random.normal(loc=50, scale=10, size=100),
'Feature_B': np.random.normal(loc=100, scale=20, size=100),
})

# Add some outliers to the dataset
data.iloc[5, 0] = 500
data.iloc[20, 1] = 200
data.iloc[35, 1] = 250

# Function to detect and remove outliers using IQR method
```

```python
def remove_outliers_iqr(data, threshold=1.5):
    Q1 = data.quantile(0.25)
    Q3 = data.quantile(0.75)
    IQR = Q3 - Q1
    filtered_data = data[~((data < (Q1 - threshold * IQR)) | (data > (Q3 + threshold * IQR))).any(axis=1)]
    return filtered_data, data[~data.index.isin(filtered_data.index)]


# Detect and remove outliers using IQR method
filtered_data = remove_outliers_iqr(data)
```

In the above code section, we are creating a sample dataset called "data" with two features, "Feature_A" and "Feature_B," containing 100 data points each. Then, we intentionally introduce outliers in the 6th and 21st rows of "Feature_A" and the 36th row of "Feature_B."

The purpose here is to detect and remove outliers using the Interquartile Range (IQR) method. The IQR is a statistical measure that represents the range between the 25th and 75th percentiles of the data distribution. Outliers are detected by calculating the lower and upper bounds as 1.5 times the IQR away from the first quartile (Q1) and third quartile (Q3), respectively. Any data points that fall below the lower bound or above the upper bound are considered outliers and are removed from the dataset.

The filtered_data DataFrame will contain the original data with the outliers removed. This method helps ensure the accuracy and reliability of data analysis by eliminating extreme values that may have resulted from errors or rare occurrences in the data.

Feature Selection

Feature selection is a critical step in the process of preparing data for analysis and modelling. It refers to the task of choosing the most relevant and informative features (also known as variables or attributes) from a dataset to build a model.

In many real-world datasets, there might be a large number of features, but not all of them contribute equally to the predictive power of the model. Some features may be redundant or have little impact on the target variable, while others could be highly informative.

Feature selection aims to identify and retain the most important features, thereby reducing the complexity of the data and improving the model's performance, interpretability, and generalization ability.

Selecting the best features involves careful examination and evaluation of the dataset to determine which features have the most significant impact on the target variable. There are several popular techniques for feature selection:

- Univariate Feature Selection: This method evaluates each feature independently and selects the top features based on statistical tests like ANOVA or chi-squared tests.

- Recursive Feature Elimination (RFE): RFE is an iterative technique that recursively removes the least important features from the dataset and ranks them based on their impact on the model's performance.

- Feature Importance from Trees: Decision tree-based algorithms like Random Forest or Gradient Boosting can provide feature importances, helping to select the most informative features.

- Correlation Analysis: This method examines the correlation between features and the target variable, and between features themselves, to retain only the most relevant ones.

- L1 Regularization (Lasso): L1 regularization penalizes less important features and encourages sparsity, making it a feature selection technique.

Let's implement the Univariate Feature Selection technique using Python:

```python
import numpy as np
import pandas as pd
from sklearn.datasets import load_breast_cancer
from sklearn.feature_selection import SelectKBest, f_classif

# Load the Breast Cancer Wisconsin (Diagnostic) dataset
data = load_breast_cancer()
X = pd.DataFrame(data.data, columns=data.feature_names)
y = data.target

# Select the top 5 features using Univariate Feature Selection
k = 5  # Set the number of top features you want to select
selector = SelectKBest(score_func=f_classif, k=k)
X_selected = selector.fit_transform(X, y)

# Get the indices of the selected features
selected_indices = np.argsort(selector.scores_)[::-1][:k]
selected_features = X.columns[selected_indices]

# Print the selected features
print("Selected Features:")
print(selected_features)
```

Selected Features: Index(['worst concave points', 'worst perimeter', 'mean concave points', 'worst radius', 'mean perimeter'], dtype='object')

Here we are using the Breast Cancer Wisconsin dataset. The dataset contains 30 features such as mean radius, mean texture, mean smoothness, and more, representing different properties of cell nuclei. The target variable is the diagnosis of breast cancer, where 0 indicates Malignant and 1 indicates Benign. We then apply the Univariate Feature Selection technique using SelectKBest and f_classif on this dataset to select the top 5 features with the highest scores. The output provides the names of the selected features, which are the five most informative attributes from the Breast Cancer Wisconsin dataset according to this feature selection method.

Principal Component Analysis

Principal Component Analysis (PCA) is a widely used dimensionality reduction technique in the field of data analysis and machine learning. It is used to simplify the complexity of high-dimensional data by transforming it into a lower-dimensional space while retaining as much of the original information as possible.

PCA identifies the most significant patterns and structures in the data by finding the principal components, which are new orthogonal (uncorrelated) variables that are a linear combination of the original features. These principal components are ordered in terms of the amount of variance they capture in the data. The first principal component explains the most significant variance, the second one explains the second-most significant variance, and so on.

PCA is particularly useful for visualizing high-dimensional data, removing redundant features, and improving the performance of machine learning models.

Below are the variants of PCA you should know:

- Standard PCA: This is the conventional PCA, which involves the computation of the principal components directly from the original data matrix.

- Incremental PCA: Incremental PCA is used when the dataset is too large to fit into memory at once. It processes data in batches and incrementally computes the principal components.

- Kernel PCA: Kernel PCA is an extension of PCA that allows for nonlinear dimensionality reduction. It employs the "kernel trick" to project data into a higher-dimensional space where it becomes linearly separable, and then PCA is applied in that space.

Let's have a look at the implementation of PCA using Python:

```python
import numpy as np
import pandas as pd
from sklearn.decomposition import PCA
import matplotlib.pyplot as plt

# Create a high-dimensional dataset with 1000 samples and 50 features
np.random.seed(42)
n_samples = 1000
n_features = 50
X_high_dim = np.random.rand(n_samples, n_features)

# Perform PCA with two principal components
n_components = 2
pca = PCA(n_components=n_components)
X_pca = pca.fit_transform(X_high_dim)
```

In the above code, we first generated a high-dimensional dataset and then apply PCA to reduce its dimensionality to two principal components. X_pca = pca.fit_transform(X_high_dim) applies PCA to the high-dimensional dataset X_high_dim. The fit_transform method performs the dimensionality reduction, transforming the original dataset into the lower-dimensional space defined by the first two principal components (n_components = 2). The result is stored in the variable X_pca.

Now let's create a figure with two subplots to compare the original data and the PCA-reduced data visually:

```python
# Create figure and axes for subplots
fig, axs = plt.subplots(1, 2, figsize=(12, 6))

# Plot the original high-dimensional data
axs[0].scatter(X_high_dim[:, 0], X_high_dim[:, 1], c='blue', alpha=0.5)
axs[0].set_xlabel('Feature 1')
axs[0].set_ylabel('Feature 2')
axs[0].set_title('Original High-Dimensional Data')

# Plot the PCA-reduced data
axs[1].scatter(X_pca[:, 0], X_pca[:, 1], c='red', alpha=0.5)
```

```
axs[1].set_xlabel('Principal Component 1')
axs[1].set_ylabel('Principal Component 2')
axs[1].set_title('PCA-Reduced Data')

# Show the subplots
plt.tight_layout()
plt.show()
```

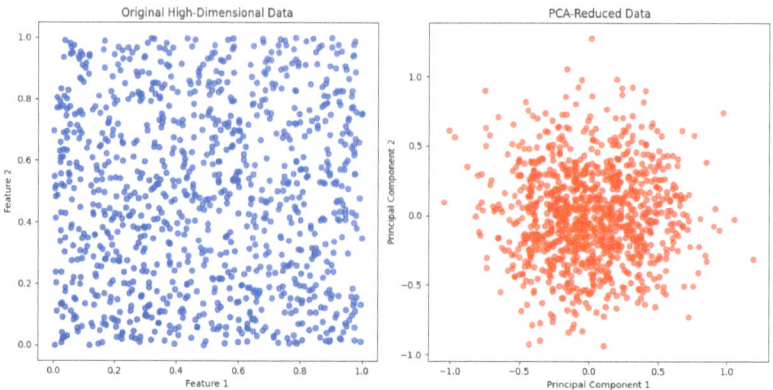

The first subplot shows the distribution of the high-dimensional data, while the second subplot will display how the data looks after PCA transformation.

Feature Scaling

Feature scaling is a preprocessing technique used to standardize or normalize the range of features in a dataset. When dealing with data that contains features with varying scales (e.g., some features with large values and others with small values), it can cause issues for certain machine learning algorithms. Feature scaling aims to bring all features to a similar scale, ensuring that no single feature dominates the learning process due to its large values.

This process does not change the underlying relationships between features but enhances the performance and convergence of machine learning algorithms during training.

There are two common feature scaling techniques:

- Standardization (Z-score normalization): This method scales the features so that they have a mean of 0 and a standard deviation of 1. It involves subtracting the mean of the feature from each data point and then dividing it by the standard deviation. Standardization is suitable when features have different units and scales.

- Normalization (Min-Max scaling): Normalization scales the features to a specified range, usually between 0 and 1. It involves subtracting the minimum value of the feature from each data point and then dividing it by the range (the difference between the maximum and minimum values). Normalization is useful when the features have a bounded range and need to be constrained within a specific scale.

Let's implement Standardization and Normalization using Python:

```python
import numpy as np
import pandas as pd
from sklearn.preprocessing import StandardScaler, MinMaxScaler

# Create a sample dataframe with features
data = pd.DataFrame({
    'Feature_A': [10, 20, 30, 40, 50],
    'Feature_B': [100, 200, 300, 400, 500],
    'Feature_C': [2, 4, 6, 8, 10]
})

# Standardization
scaler_standard = StandardScaler()
X_standardized = scaler_standard.fit_transform(data)

# Normalization
scaler_minmax = MinMaxScaler()
X_normalized = scaler_minmax.fit_transform(X)

# Print the first few rows of the scaled data
print("Original Data:")
print(X.head())
```

```
print("\nStandardized Data:")
print(pd.DataFrame(X_standardized, columns=data.columns).head())

print("\nNormalized Data:")
print(pd.DataFrame(X_normalized, columns=X.columns).head())
```

In this code, I've created a sample dataframe named data with three features: 'Feature_A', 'Feature_B', and 'Feature_C'. The values in each feature are arbitrary for demonstration purposes. The StandardScaler and MinMaxScaler are used to scale the features using Standardization and Normalization, respectively.

```
Original Data:
   Feature_A  Feature_B
0         10        100
1         20        200
2         30        300
3         40        400
4         50        500

Standardized Data:
   Feature_A  Feature_B  Feature_C
0  -1.414214  -1.414214  -1.414214
1  -0.707107  -0.707107  -0.707107
2   0.000000   0.000000   0.000000
3   0.707107   0.707107   0.707107
4   1.414214   1.414214   1.414214

Normalized Data:
   Feature_A  Feature_B
0       0.00       0.00
1       0.25       0.25
2       0.50       0.50
3       0.75       0.75
4       1.00       1.00
```

It is important to note that we should never scale the target variable when performing feature scaling in data preprocessing for machine learning tasks. The reason behind this is that scaling the target variable can introduce unintended biases and distort the true nature of the target's distribution, leading to inaccurate model predictions.

The primary purpose of feature scaling is to bring all the features to a similar scale to facilitate the convergence and performance of machine learning algorithms during training. However, the target variable represents the outcome we want to predict, and its scale holds essential information about the problem we are trying to solve. Altering the target variable's scale could affect the model's ability to learn and predict accurately.

Moreover, scaling the target variable may cause the predictions to be outside the original range, making them meaningless or difficult to interpret. For instance, in regression tasks, scaling the target variable may lead to predictions that are scaled versions of the original target values, which could be misleading when interpreting the model's results.

Hyperparameter Tuning

Hyperparameter tuning, also known as hyperparameter optimization, is the process of finding the best set of hyperparameters for a machine learning model. Hyperparameters are configuration settings of a model that are set before the training process begins and remain fixed during training. Unlike model parameters, which are learned from the data, hyperparameters need to be determined beforehand, and their values can significantly impact the model's performance.

Hyperparameter tuning aims to search through different combinations of hyperparameter values to find the optimal configuration that maximizes the model's performance on the validation set. The goal is to strike a balance between underfitting (where the model is too simple to capture the complexity of the data) and overfitting (where the model memorizes the training data but fails to generalize to unseen data).

There are several techniques for hyperparameter tuning, including:

Grid Search: Grid search involves defining a grid of possible hyperparameter values and evaluating the model's performance for all possible combinations within the grid. It can be computationally expensive but exhaustive in searching the hyperparameter space.

Random Search: Random search randomly samples hyperparameter values from predefined ranges, reducing the computational cost compared to grid search. It explores a more diverse set of hyperparameter combinations and may find good solutions faster.

Let's implement Grid Search and Random Search using Python:

```python
import numpy as np
import pandas as pd
from sklearn.model_selection import GridSearchCV, RandomizedSearchCV
from sklearn.ensemble import RandomForestClassifier
from sklearn.datasets import load_iris

# Load the Iris dataset
data = load_iris()
X = data.data
y = data.target

# Define the hyperparameter grid for Grid Search
param_grid = {
    'n_estimators': [50, 100, 150],
    'max_depth': [None, 5, 10],
    'min_samples_split': [2, 5, 10],
}

# Perform Grid Search with Random Forest Classifier
rf_classifier = RandomForestClassifier()
grid_search = GridSearchCV(rf_classifier, param_grid, cv=3)
grid_search.fit(X, y)

# Print the best hyperparameter values from Grid Search
print("Best Hyperparameters from Grid Search:")
print(grid_search.best_params_)

# Perform Random Search with Random Forest Classifier
random_search = RandomizedSearchCV(rf_classifier,
                                   param_distributions=param_grid,
                                   n_iter=10, cv=3)
random_search.fit(X, y)

# Print the best hyperparameter values from Random Search
print("\nBest Hyperparameters from Random Search:")
print(random_search.best_params_)
```

```
Best Hyperparameters from Grid Search: {'max_depth': 5,
'min_samples_split': 5, 'n_estimators': 50}

Best Hyperparameters from Random Search: {'n_estimators': 150,
'min_samples_split': 5, 'max_depth': None}
```

In this code, we use the Iris dataset and perform Grid Search and Random Search with a Random Forest Classifier. We define a hyperparameter grid param_grid with different values for 'n_estimators', 'max_depth', and 'min_samples_split'. Grid Search exhaustively searches through all combinations in the grid, while Random Search randomly samples combinations from the grid. The best hyperparameter values found by each search method are printed to determine the optimal configuration for the Random Forest Classifier on the Iris dataset.

SMOTE

SMOTE (Synthetic Minority Over-sampling Technique) is a resampling technique used to address the issue of imbalanced class distributions in a dataset. It is specifically designed to handle imbalanced binary classification problems where one class is significantly under-represented compared to the other.

SMOTE generates synthetic samples for the minority class by creating new data points that lie along the line segments connecting similar instances from the minority class. These synthetic samples help balance the class distribution and prevent the model from being biased towards the majority class during training.

SMOTE is applied when dealing with imbalanced datasets, where the target variable has a large class imbalance. In such cases, traditional machine learning algorithms may struggle to properly classify the minority class, leading to poor predictive performance. By generating synthetic samples for the minority class, SMOTE creates a more balanced training set, enabling the model to learn from both classes effectively and improve its ability to generalize to unseen data.

To implement SMOTE using Python, you need to install the Python' imbalance-learn library. You can install it by executing the pip command mentioned below in your terminal or command prompt:

`pip install imbalanced-learn`

Now here's how to implement SMOTE using Python:

```python
import numpy as np
import pandas as pd
from imblearn.over_sampling import SMOTE

# Create a sample imbalanced dataset with two classes (0 and 1)
np.random.seed(42)
X = np.random.rand(100, 2)
y = np.array([0] * 90 + [1] * 10)

# Apply SMOTE to generate synthetic samples for the minority class
smote = SMOTE(sampling_strategy='auto')
X_resampled, y_resampled = smote.fit_resample(X, y)

# Print the class distribution after SMOTE
print("Class Distribution after SMOTE:")
print(pd.Series(y_resampled).value_counts())


Class Distribution after SMOTE:
0  90
1  90
dtype: int64
```

In this code, we created a sample imbalanced dataset with two classes (0 and 1). We then applied SMOTE using SMOTE from the imbalanced-learn library to generate synthetic samples for the minority class. The sampling_strategy parameter is set to 'auto', which ensures that the number of synthetic samples created is equal to the number of samples in the majority class, thereby balancing the class distribution. The class distribution after applying SMOTE is printed to demonstrate the effect of the technique on balancing the class distribution.

Summary

In this chapter, we delved into the crucial data preprocessing elements that play a pivotal role in training better machine learning models. We began by addressing the challenge of missing values in our data. Next, we tackled outliers, which can significantly impact the performance of our models. Feature selection emerged as another critical aspect of data preprocessing. We explored various methods to identify the most informative features in our dataset, allowing our models to focus on the most relevant information and disregard irrelevant noise.

Principal Component Analysis (PCA) was a powerful technique we examined to reduce the dimensionality of our data. By transforming our features into a more concise representation, PCA enabled us to maintain critical information while minimizing computational complexity. Additionally, we learned the importance of feature scaling, where we standardized our features to a common scale. Hyperparameter tuning was yet another vital element explored in this chapter. Lastly, we addressed the challenge of class imbalance with the Synthetic Minority Over-sampling Technique (SMOTE).

Overall, this chapter provided us with a comprehensive understanding of essential data preprocessing techniques. By mastering these crucial elements, we equipped ourselves with the tools to prepare our data effectively and build more powerful Machine Learning models capable of making accurate and reliable predictions.

Chapter 11: Neural Network Architectures for Deep Learning

Introduction

Neural Networks are a class of artificial intelligence algorithms inspired by the structure and functioning of the human brain. They are a fundamental part of Machine Learning and are designed to learn and model complex relationships within data.

A neural network consists of interconnected nodes, called neurons, organized in layers: an input layer, one or more hidden layers, and an output layer. Each neuron processes incoming information and applies mathematical operations to generate an output. The network's architecture allows it to process and transform data through multiple layers of computation, enabling it to extract intricate patterns and make predictions or classifications.

The design of artificial neural networks draws inspiration from the biological nervous system, particularly the human brain. In the brain, neurons are interconnected and communicate through electrical and chemical signals. When a neuron receives input signals, it processes this information and generates an output signal, which can further stimulate neighbouring neurons. This interconnectedness and parallel processing in the brain contribute to its powerful and adaptive capabilities for learning and cognition.

Similarly, in artificial neural networks, each artificial neuron receives input data and applies a set of mathematical operations to compute an output. The interconnections between neurons allow information to flow through the network, and the strength of these connections (weights) determines how much influence each neuron has on the overall computation. By iteratively adjusting these weights during training, the neural network learns to optimize its performance on a specific task, such as image recognition or natural language processing.

The Computational Structure of Neural Networks

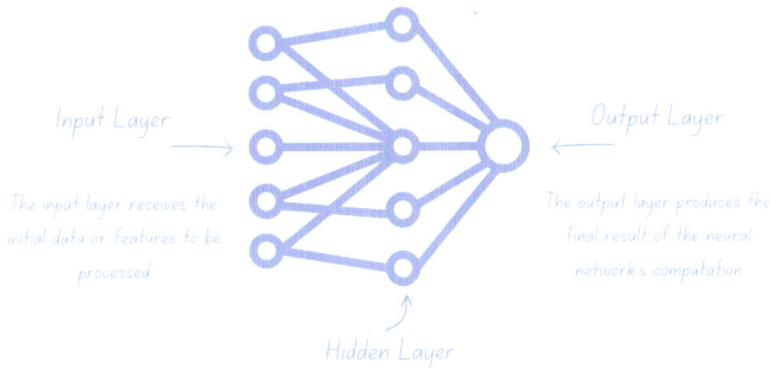

A neural network is a computational model inspired by the functioning of the human brain. It consists of interconnected nodes, called neurons, organized in multiple layers. The structure of a neural network typically includes:

- an input layer;
- one or more hidden layers;
- an output layer;

The input layer receives the initial data or features to be processed. Each neuron in the input layer corresponds to a specific input feature and serves as the starting point for information flow.

The hidden layers, located between the input and output layers, perform computations on the data. Each neuron in the hidden layers receives inputs from the previous layer, applies mathematical operations, and passes the results to the next layer. The number of hidden layers and neurons within each layer can vary depending on the complexity of the task.

The output layer produces the final result of the neural network's computation. Each neuron in the output layer represents a specific output or prediction. The information flows from the input layer through the hidden layers to the output layer, with computations and transformations occurring at each stage.

Connections between neurons are known as weights. Weights determine the strength of influence one neuron has on another. These weights are adjusted during the learning process of the neural network to optimize its performance. Activation functions are applied to the weighted sums of inputs in each neuron, introducing non-linearities and enabling the network to learn complex patterns and make predictions.

How Neural Networks Work?

At its core, a neural network contains interconnected nodes called neurons. These neurons are organized into layers: an input layer, one or more hidden layers, and an output layer. Each neuron is associated with a weight, representing the strength of the connection between neurons.

The process of training a neural network involves two main steps:

1. forward propagation
2. and backpropagation

During forward propagation, input data is fed into the network and flows through the layers. Each neuron in the input layer receives an input value and passes it to the neurons in the first hidden layer. Each connection between neurons is assigned a weight, which is multiplied by the input value. These weighted inputs are summed up, and a bias term (a constant) is added to introduce flexibility.

The weighted sum is then passed through an activation function, which introduces non-linearity into the network. The activation function determines whether the neuron should be activated or not, based on the input it receives.

The output of the activation function becomes the input of that particular neuron and is then it's passed to the next layer. This process continues until the output layer is reached, where the final result or prediction of the neural network is received.

Backpropagation adjusts the weights based on the difference between the predicted and desired output. It calculates the error at the output layer and propagates it backwards through the network. The weights are updated using gradient descent, taking the derivative of the error with respect to each weight. The weights are adjusted in the opposite direction of the gradient, aiming to minimize the error. This process is repeated iteratively, refining the network's weights to improve predictions.

This iterative process of forward propagation and backpropagation continues for a set number of epochs or until the network reaches a satisfactory level of accuracy.

The structure of a neural network allows it to learn and adapt to different tasks by adjusting the weights and biases associated with the connections. They can iteratively improve their performance by comparing their predictions with the desired outputs and adjusting the weights accordingly. That is why Neural networks are widely used despite the existence of other machine learning algorithms due to their unique capabilities.

Neural networks can learn complex patterns and relationships in data, even when the relationships are non-linear or abstract. They can automatically extract relevant features from raw data, eliminating the need for manual feature engineering. Additionally, neural networks are highly flexible and can adapt to different problem domains and data types. Their ability to model and approximate any arbitrary function makes them powerful tools for a wide range of tasks, such as image and speech recognition, natural language processing, and predictive modelling. Therefore, the use of neural networks is justified by their ability to handle complex and diverse data flexibly and powerfully, which sets them apart from other machine learning algorithms.

Getting Started with Perceptron

The Perceptron is a fundamental building block of artificial neural networks. It is a type of artificial neuron designed to mimic the basic functionality of a biological neuron. The Perceptron takes multiple inputs, each multiplied by a corresponding weight, and sums up these weighted inputs. It then applies an activation function to the sum to produce an output. The activation function determines whether the neuron should fire (produce an output of 1) or remain inactive (produce an output of 0) based on the summed input.

Single-layer networks, like the Perceptron, have limitations when it comes to learning complex patterns and relationships in data. They can only learn linearly separable patterns, which means they can only classify data points that can be separated by a straight line or plane in the input space. If the data is not linearly separable, a single-layer network like the Perceptron cannot learn the correct decision boundary, resulting in poor performance.

In the Perceptron, the activation function is a key component that introduces non-linearity to the model's computations. The original Perceptron used the step function as its activation function, where the output was 1 if the sum of weighted inputs was positive, and 0 otherwise. However, the step function's discontinuity makes it unsuitable for training with gradient-based optimization algorithms.

Common activation functions used in modern Perceptrons include:

- Step Function (Binary Step): Outputs 1 if the sum of weighted inputs is positive, otherwise 0. (Not commonly used in modern neural networks).

- Sigmoid Function: Squashes the input into a range between 0 and 1, making it suitable for probabilistic interpretations and binary classification problems.

- ReLU (Rectified Linear Unit): Outputs the input directly if it is positive, otherwise 0. ReLU has become popular due to its simplicity and effectiveness in training deep neural networks.

- Tanh Function (Hyperbolic Tangent): Squashes the input into a range between -1 and 1, similar to the Sigmoid but with a centred mean.

Let's implement a simple Perceptron using Python:

```python
import numpy as np

class Perceptron:
    def __init__(self, input_dim):
        self.weights = np.random.rand(input_dim)
```

```
        self.bias = np.random.rand()

    def predict(self, inputs):
        weighted_sum = np.dot(inputs, self.weights) + self.bias
        return 1 if weighted_sum >= 0 else 0

# Example usage:
input_data = np.array([1, 0, 1])
perceptron = Perceptron(input_dim=len(input_data))
prediction = perceptron.predict(input_data)
print("Prediction:", prediction)
```

```
Prediction: 1
```

In this code, we defined a simple Perceptron class with an __init__ method to initialize random weights and a bias. The predict method takes input data as a NumPy array, computes the weighted sum of inputs, and applies the step activation function to make a binary prediction (1 or 0).

This is a basic implementation of a Perceptron, and its limitations include the inability to learn non-linear patterns and handle more complex data. To address these limitations, we need to use multi-layer networks like deep neural networks.

Multi-layer Perceptrons

Multi-layer Perceptrons (MLPs) are a type of artificial neural network that consists of multiple layers of interconnected neurons. Each layer in the network serves a specific purpose. The input layer receives the input data, and the output layer produces the final prediction or output. In between the input and output layers, there are one or more hidden layers, where the real computation and learning take place.

Each neuron in the hidden layers receives input from the previous layer, applies a set of weighted computations, and passes the output to the next layer. The connections between neurons have associated weights that are adjusted during the training process to optimize the network's performance on the task at hand.

The feedforward process in MLPs refers to the flow of information through the network from the input layer to the output layer. It is called "feedforward" because the data flows only in one direction, without any feedback loops.

During the feedforward process, each layer's neurons process the input data and pass the output to the next layer. This process continues until the output layer produces the final prediction or output. The activations (outputs) of the neurons in each layer depend on the weighted inputs and the activation function applied to them. The feedforward process is used for making predictions or classifications based on the learned weights of the network.

Backpropagation is an essential algorithm used in training multi-layer neural networks, including MLPs. The goal of training a neural network is to minimize the error between the predicted output and the actual target output. Backpropagation helps in adjusting the weights of the network to reduce this error. The algorithm works by propagating the error backwards from the output layer to the hidden layers and eventually to the input layer. It calculates the gradient of the error with respect to the network's weights, allowing the weights to be updated in the direction that minimizes the error. By iteratively applying backpropagation to the training data, the network learns to improve its predictions and adapt to the underlying patterns in the data.

Activation functions are an essential component of MLPs as they introduce non-linearity to the model's computations. Without non-linearity, the network would behave like a linear model, limiting its ability to learn complex patterns in the data. Activation functions determine whether a neuron should be activated (produce an output) based on the weighted sum of its inputs.

Common activation functions used in MLPs include:

- Sigmoid Function: This function maps the weighted sum of inputs to a value between 0 and 1. It is often used in the output layer for binary classification problems.

- Tanh Function (Hyperbolic Tangent): Similar to the sigmoid function, but it maps the weighted sum of inputs to a value between -1 and 1. Tanh is often used in hidden layers and is effective for problems with symmetrically distributed data.

- ReLU (Rectified Linear Unit): ReLU outputs the weighted sum directly if it is positive, and 0 otherwise. ReLU has gained popularity due to its simplicity and faster convergence during training.

- Leaky ReLU: An improved version of ReLU that allows a small non-zero output when the weighted sum is negative. This helps to overcome some issues related to "dying ReLU" during training.

- Softmax Function: Softmax is used in the output layer for multi-class classification problems. It converts the weighted sum of inputs into probabilities, making it suitable for choosing the most likely class among multiple classes.

Let's implement a simple MLP using Python and the popular Deep Learning library, Keras:

```python
import numpy as np
from keras.models import Sequential
from keras.layers import Dense

# Create a sample dataset
np.random.seed(42)
X = np.random.rand(100, 10) # 100 samples, 10 features
y = np.random.randint(2, size=100) # Binary labels (0 or 1)

# Create an MLP model
```

```
model = Sequential()
model.add(Dense(32, activation='relu', input_dim=10)) # Hidden layer with 32 neurons
and ReLU activation

model.add(Dense(1, activation='sigmoid')) # Output layer with 1 neuron and Sigmoid
activation

# Compile the model
model.compile(optimizer='adam', loss='binary_crossentropy', metrics=['accuracy'])

# Train the model
model.fit(X, y, epochs=10, batch_size=32)
```

In this code, we first created a sample dataset with 100 samples and 10 features. Then, we defined an MLP model using Keras, consisting of a hidden layer with 32 neurons and ReLU activation, and an output layer with 1 neuron and Sigmoid activation. We compile the model with the Adam optimizer and binary cross-entropy loss function, suitable for binary classification. Finally, we train the model on the data for 10 epochs using a batch size of 32. The trained model can then be used to make predictions on new data.

Convolutional Neural Networks

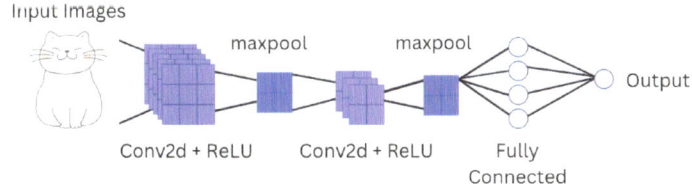

A Convolutional Neural Network (CNN) is a specialized type of artificial neural network designed to process and analyze visual data, such as images and videos. CNNs are widely used in computer vision tasks due to their ability to automatically learn hierarchical features from raw pixel values. They are particularly effective in image recognition, object detection, image segmentation, and various other tasks related to visual understanding.

The structure of a Convolutional Neural Network consists of several layers, each serving a specific purpose in the image processing pipeline:

- Convolutional Layers: These layers are the core of CNNs and consist of multiple learnable filters or kernels. Each filter is a small matrix that slides over the input image, scanning it for relevant patterns. The convolution operation involves element-wise multiplication of the filter and the corresponding image region, followed by summation. This process generates feature maps that represent the presence of specific patterns or features in different parts of the image.

- Activation Layers: After the convolution operation, an activation function (usually ReLU) is applied to introduce non-linearity to the model, allowing it to capture complex patterns effectively.

- Pooling Layers: Pooling layers downsample the feature maps, reducing their spatial dimensions and the number of parameters. Max pooling is commonly used, which retains the maximum value within a small window, effectively preserving the most important features.

- Fully Connected Layers: These layers are similar to those in traditional neural networks and serve to perform classification or regression tasks based on the learned features from the previous layers.

Convolutional Neural Networks (CNNs) are designed to automatically identify patterns and features in visual data, like images. They start with an input image and use convolutional layers with small filters to detect specific patterns by scanning the image. The results create new feature maps that highlight different patterns. Activation functions introduce non-linearity, pooling layers downsample the maps, and stacking multiple layers allows the network to learn more complex features. Fully connected layers then perform classification tasks, and during training, the network adjusts its filter weights and biases through backpropagation to improve performance. Overall, CNNs excel at image recognition and understanding visual data by progressively learning more abstract features from the input images.

Let's implement a simple CNN for image classification using Python and Keras:

```python
import numpy as np
import keras
from keras.models import Sequential
from keras.layers import Conv2D, MaxPooling2D, Flatten, Dense

# Create a sample dataset
np.random.seed(42)

# 100 images of size 28x28 with 3 color channels
X = np.random.rand(100, 28, 28, 3)
y = np.random.randint(10, size=100) # Labels for 10 classes (0 to 9)

# Create a CNN model
model = Sequential()

# Convolutional layer with 32 filters and ReLU activation
model.add(Conv2D(32, kernel_size=(3, 3), activation='relu', input_shape=(28, 28, 3)))
model.add(MaxPooling2D(pool_size=(2, 2))) # Max pooling layer

model.add(Flatten()) # Flatten the output for fully connected layers

# Fully connected output layer with 10 neurons for 10 classes and Softmax activation
model.add(Dense(10, activation='softmax'))

# Compile the model
model.compile(optimizer='adam', loss='sparse_categorical_crossentropy', metrics=['accuracy'])

# Train the model
model.fit(X, y, epochs=10, batch_size=32)
```

In this code, we first created a sample dataset of 100 images of size 28x28 with 3 colour channels (RGB). Then, we define a CNN model using Keras, consisting of a convolutional layer with 32 filters, followed by a max pooling layer. The output of these layers is then flattened and passed to a fully connected output layer with 10 neurons (for 10 classes) and Softmax activation. The model is compiled with the Adam optimizer and sparse categorical cross-entropy loss function, suitable for multi-class classification. Finally, we train the model on the data for 10 epochs using a batch size of 32. The trained model can then be used to make predictions on new images.

Recurrent Neural Networks

A Recurrent Neural Network (RNN) is a type of artificial neural network designed to process sequential data. Unlike traditional feedforward neural networks, RNNs have connections that create loops, allowing information to persist and be passed from one step to the next. This looping behaviour enables RNNs to capture temporal dependencies and patterns in sequences, making them well-suited for tasks like natural language processing, speech recognition, and time series analysis.

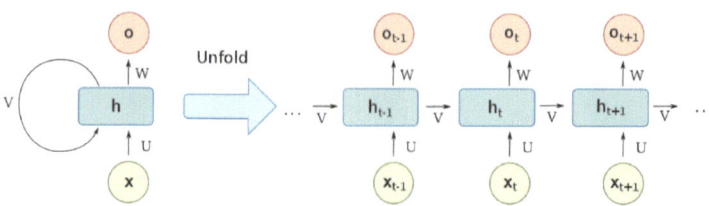

The structure of a Recurrent Neural Network can be represented as a series of interconnected hidden states, where each hidden state represents the network's memory at a particular time step. RNNs process sequential data in the following manner:

- Input Sequence: At each time step t, the RNN receives an input vector representing the data at that time step. For example, in natural language processing, each time step may correspond to a word or a character in a sentence.

- Hidden State: The RNN maintains a hidden state vector at each time step, which serves as its memory. The hidden state captures the information from the current input and the previous hidden state, allowing the network to remember past information.

- Recurrent Connection: The key feature of RNNs is the recurrent connection, which connects the hidden state of the one-time step to the next time step. This looping connection enables the network to share information across different time steps, making it capable of understanding the sequential nature of the data.

- Output: The RNN can produce an output at each time step based on the corresponding hidden state. For example, in language modelling tasks, the RNN can predict the next word in a sentence based on the previous words and their hidden states.

At the start of the sequence, the RNN's hidden state is initialized to a fixed vector or set to zeros. As the input sequence is presented one-time step at a time, the RNN updates its hidden state using the current input and the previous hidden state. This process is repeated for each time step, allowing the network to process the entire sequence. The recurrent connection in the RNN allows information to flow from one time step to the next, creating a memory of past inputs. This looping behaviour enables the RNN to capture long-range dependencies and patterns in the sequence. This is how a Recurrent Neural Network Architecture works. The RNN can produce an output at each time step or only at the final time step. The output is often used for various tasks, such as sequence generation, classification, or regression.

Let's implement a simple RNN using Python and Keras:

```python
import numpy as np
import keras
from keras.models import Sequential
from keras.layers import SimpleRNN, Dense

# Create a sample sequential data
np.random.seed(42)

# 100 sequences of length 10 with 1 feature
X = np.random.rand(100, 10, 1)
y = np.random.randint(2, size=100) # Binary labels (0 or 1)

# Create an RNN model
model = Sequential()

# RNN layer with 32 neurons
model.add(SimpleRNN(32, input_shape=(10, 1)))

# Output layer with 1 neuron for binary classification and Sigmoid activation
model.add(Dense(1, activation='sigmoid'))
# Compile the model
model.compile(optimizer='adam', loss='binary_crossentropy', metrics=['accuracy'])

# Train the model
model.fit(X, y, epochs=10, batch_size=32)
```

In this code, we first created a sample dataset of 100 sequences, each of length 10 with 1 feature. Then, we defined an RNN model using Keras, consisting of a SimpleRNN layer with 32 neurons. The output of the RNN layer is passed to a fully connected output layer with 1 neuron for binary classification. The model is compiled with the Adam optimizer and binary cross-entropy loss function, suitable for binary classification. Finally, we train the model on the data for 10 epochs using a batch size of 32. The trained RNN can then be used to make predictions on new sequential data.

Long Short-Term Memory Networks

Long Short-Term Memory (LSTM) Networks are a type of Recurrent Neural Network (RNN) that is designed to overcome the vanishing and exploding gradient problems in traditional RNNs. LSTMs are well-suited for processing sequential data with long-term dependencies, such as natural language, speech, and time series data. They utilize specialized memory cells and gating mechanisms to selectively retain and forget information over time, allowing them to capture relevant patterns and information across long sequences.

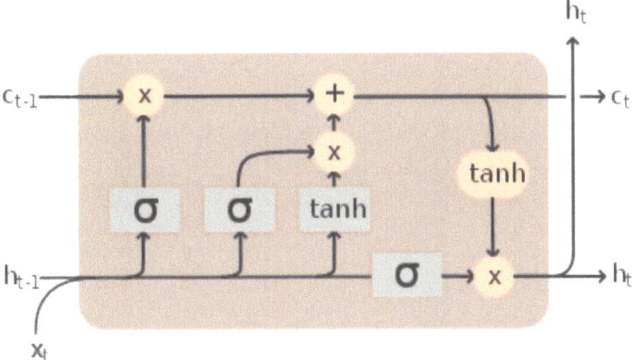

The structure of an LSTM can be understood as a sequence of memory cells, each equipped with three gating mechanisms that control the flow of information:

- Input Gate: The input gate determines which parts of the input should be stored in the memory cell. It takes into account the current input and the previous hidden state and outputs a value between 0 and 1 for each input element, indicating the relevance of the input for the current memory cell.

- Forget Gate: The forget gate determines which information in the memory cell should be discarded. It takes into account the current input and the previous hidden state and outputs a value between 0 and 1 for each element in the memory cell, indicating the importance of retaining the information.

- Output Gate: The output gate determines what information from the memory cell should be passed to the next time step. It takes into account the current input and the previous hidden state and outputs a value between 0 and 1 for each element in the memory cell, indicating the contribution of the information to the final output.

The LSTM memory cell itself operates in the following steps:

- Input Processing: The input gate and the current input are used to update the memory cell's contents with relevant information from the input.

- Forget Processing: The forget gate and the previous memory cell contents are used to decide which information needs to be discarded from the memory cell.

- Output Processing: The output gate and the updated memory cell contents are used to compute the output of the LSTM for the current time step.

At the start of the sequence, the LSTM's hidden state and memory cell are initialized to fixed vectors or set to zeros. As the input sequence is presented one-time step at a time, the LSTM updates its hidden state and memory cell using the input and the previous hidden state. The gating mechanisms (input gate, forget gate, and output gate) control the flow of information into and out of the memory cell, selectively retaining and forgetting information as needed. The design of LSTMs allows them to capture long-term dependencies in the sequence by selectively updating and retaining information in the memory cell over time. This is how LSTM neural networks work. The LSTM can produce an output at each time step or only at the final time step. The output is often used for various tasks, such as sequence generation, classification, or regression.

Let's implement a simple LSTM using Python and Keras:

```python
import numpy as np
import keras
from keras.models import Sequential
from keras.layers import LSTM, Dense

# Create a sample sequential data
np.random.seed(42)

# 100 sequences of length 10 with 1 feature
X = np.random.rand(100, 10, 1)
y = np.random.randint(2, size=100) # Binary labels (0 or 1)

# Create an LSTM model
model = Sequential()
model.add(LSTM(32, input_shape=(10, 1))) # LSTM layer with 32 neurons

# Output layer with 1 neuron for binary classification and Sigmoid activation
model.add(Dense(1, activation='sigmoid'))

# Compile the model
model.compile(optimizer='adam', loss='binary_crossentropy', metrics=['accuracy'])

# Train the model
model.fit(X, y, epochs=10, batch_size=32)
```

In this code, we first created a sample dataset of 100 sequences, each of length 10 with 1 feature. Then, we defined an LSTM model using Keras, consisting of an LSTM layer with 32 neurons. The output of the LSTM layer is passed to a fully connected output layer with 1 neuron for binary classification. The model is compiled with the Adam optimizer and binary cross-entropy loss function, suitable for binary classification. Finally, we train the model on the data for 10 epochs using a batch size of 32. The trained LSTM can then be used to make predictions on new sequential data.

Generative Adversarial Networks

Generative Adversarial Networks (GANs) are a class of deep learning models that consist of two neural networks, the generator and the discriminator, engaged in a game-like competition. GANs are used to generate new data samples that resemble a given dataset. The generator network generates fake samples, and the discriminator network evaluates whether the samples are real (from the original dataset) or fake (generated by the generator). Through this adversarial process, GANs learn to produce increasingly realistic data samples, leading to impressive results in generating images, videos, music, and other types of data.

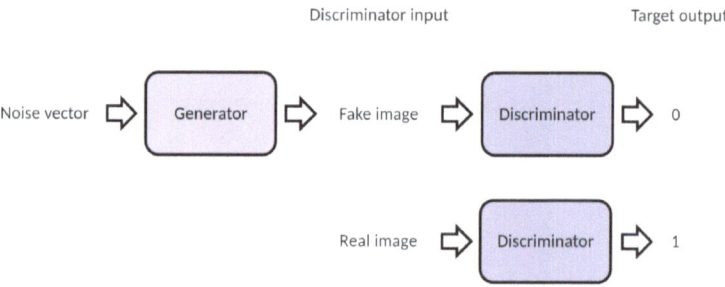

The structure of a Generative Adversarial Network involves two main components:

- Generator Network: The generator is responsible for creating fake data samples that resemble real data. It takes random noise as input and transforms it into data samples that should look like they belong to the original dataset. The generator consists of several layers that gradually transform the noise into more complex patterns, generating data samples that become increasingly realistic as the training progresses.

- Discriminator Network: The discriminator is the adversary of the generator. It acts as a binary classifier and is trained to distinguish between real data samples from the original dataset and fake data samples generated by the generator. The discriminator also consists of several layers that process the input data and make a decision about its authenticity.

Let's understand how GANs work. The generator and discriminator networks are initialized with random weights. The generator takes random noise as input and generates fake data samples. The discriminator evaluates both real data samples from the original dataset and fake data samples from the generator. It classifies them as real or fake, respectively. The generator's objective is to produce fake data samples that are indistinguishable from real data, aiming to fool the discriminator. The discriminator's objective is to correctly classify real and fake data samples.

The generator and discriminator networks are trained alternately, with the generator trying to improve its ability to generate realistic samples while the discriminator tries to become more accurate in distinguishing real from fake samples.

The generator and discriminator networks engage in an adversarial game-like competition, where the generator tries to deceive the discriminator with increasingly realistic samples, and the discriminator tries to become more skilled at detecting fake samples. Over time, through this adversarial learning process, the generator becomes better at generating high-quality data samples, and the discriminator becomes more accurate in identifying real from fake samples.

Let's implement a simple Generative Adversarial Network for generating images using Python and Keras:

```
import numpy as np
import keras
from keras.models import Sequential
from keras.layers import Dense, LeakyReLU
```

```python
from keras.optimizers import Adam

# Create a sample dataset of random noise
np.random.seed(42)
# 100 samples of random noise with 100 dimensions
X_noise = np.random.rand(100, 100)

# Create a generator model
generator = Sequential()
generator.add(Dense(256, input_dim=100))
generator.add(LeakyReLU(alpha=0.01))
generator.add(Dense(512))
generator.add(LeakyReLU(alpha=0.01))
# Output layer with 784 neurons for 28x28 images
generator.add(Dense(784, activation='tanh'))

# Create a discriminator model
discriminator = Sequential()
discriminator.add(Dense(512, input_dim=784))
discriminator.add(LeakyReLU(alpha=0.01))
discriminator.add(Dense(256))
discriminator.add(LeakyReLU(alpha=0.01))
# Output layer with 1 neuron for binary classification
discriminator.add(Dense(1, activation='sigmoid'))

# Compile the discriminator
discriminator.compile(optimizer=Adam(learning_rate=0.0002, beta_1=0.5),
loss='binary_crossentropy')

# Create a GAN model by combining the generator and discriminator
discriminator.trainable = False # Freeze the discriminator during GAN training
gan = Sequential()
gan.add(generator)
gan.add(discriminator)

# Compile the GAN
gan.compile(optimizer=Adam(learning_rate=0.0002, beta_1=0.5),
loss='binary_crossentropy')
```

In this code, we first created a sample dataset of random noise (100 samples of random noise with 100 dimensions). Then, we defined the generator and discriminator models using Keras. The generator takes random noise as input and produces 28x28 image-like data samples as output. The discriminator is trained to distinguish between real images (from the original dataset) and fake images (generated by the generator).

Next, we compiled the discriminator using the binary cross-entropy loss function. Then, we create a GAN model by combining the generator and discriminator. During GAN training, we freeze the discriminator to prevent it from updating its weights. We then compiled the GAN model.

And here's how you can train the GAN model:

```python
# 1000 samples of real images with 784 dimensions (28x28 images flattened)
X_real = np.random.rand(1000, 784)

# Fit the GAN model
epochs = 10000
batch_size = 64

for epoch in range(epochs):
    # Generate fake images using the generator
    noise = np.random.rand(batch_size, 100)
    fake_images = generator.predict(noise)
    # Select a random batch of real images from the original dataset
    idx = np.random.randint(0, X_real.shape[0], batch_size)
    real_images = X_real[idx]
    # Concatenate real and fake images to create a batch for training the discriminator
    X_combined = np.concatenate([real_images, fake_images])
# Labels for the discriminator: 1 for real images, 0 for fake images
    y_discriminator = np.zeros(2 * batch_size)
    y_discriminator[:batch_size] = 0.9 # One-sided label smoothing for stability
    # Train the discriminator
    discriminator_loss = discriminator.train_on_batch(X_combined, y_discriminator)

    # Generate new noise for the generator
    noise = np.random.rand(batch_size, 100)
    # Labels for the generator: 1 (real) because we want the discriminator to mistake fake images as real
    y_generator = np.ones(batch_size)
    # Train the GAN (generator only)
    gan_loss = gan.train_on_batch(noise, y_generator)
    # Print the progress
    if epoch % 100 == 0:
        print(f"Epoch {epoch} | Discriminator Loss: {discriminator_loss} | GAN Loss: {gan_loss}")
```

In this code, we defined the number of epochs and the batch size for training the GAN. Then, we loop through the specified number of epochs and perform the following steps:

- Generate fake images using the generator by passing random noise as input.

- Select a random batch of real images from the original dataset.

- Concatenate the real and fake images to create a combined batch for training the discriminator.

- Create labels for the discriminator: 0.9 for real images (one-sided label smoothing for stability) and 0 for fake images.

- Train the discriminator on the combined batch of real and fake images.

- Generate new noise for the generator.

- Create labels for the generator: 1 (real) because we want the discriminator to mistake fake images for real.

- Train the GAN (generator only) on the new noise and the labels for the generator.

- Print the discriminator and GAN losses to monitor the training progress.

This loop continues for the specified number of epochs, and as the GAN trains, the generator becomes better at generating realistic images, while the discriminator becomes more accurate in distinguishing real from fake images. The goal is for the generator to produce images that are indistinguishable from real images. The training process can be time-consuming, depending on the complexity of the dataset and the models.

Transformer Networks

Transformer Networks are a type of deep learning model specifically designed for processing sequential data, such as natural language, audio, and time series data. They were introduced in the paper "Attention Is All You Need" by Vaswani et al. (2017) and have since become a cornerstone in various natural language processing tasks. Transformer Networks have revolutionized sequence-to-sequence tasks, such as machine translation and text generation, by leveraging self-attention mechanisms to efficiently capture long-range dependencies in sequences.

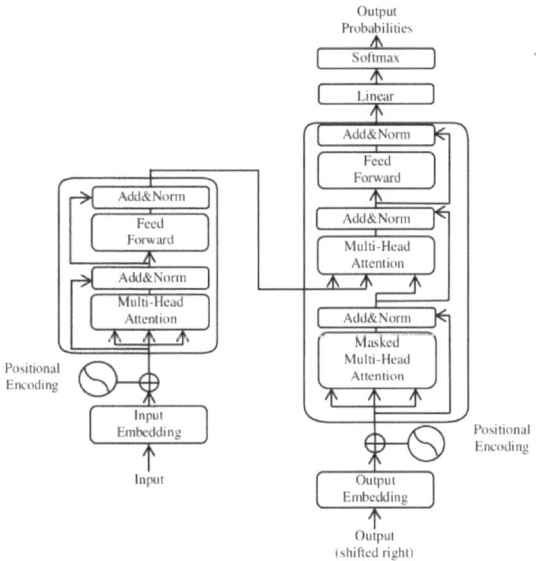

The structure of Transformer Networks is based on self-attention mechanisms, where each position in the input sequence can attend to all other positions. The key components of Transformer Networks include:

- Encoder: The encoder takes the input sequence and processes it through multiple layers of self-attention and feed-forward neural networks. The self-attention mechanism allows the model to weigh the importance of each position in the input sequence based on its relationship with all other positions. The output of the encoder is a set of context-aware representations for each position in the input sequence.

- Decoder: The decoder also consists of multiple layers of self-attention and feed-forward neural networks. It takes the output of the encoder and generates the output sequence step-by-step. During decoding, each position can only attend to previous positions in the output sequence to ensure autoregressive generation.

- Self-Attention Mechanism: The self-attention mechanism in Transformer Networks allows each position in the sequence to attend to all other positions, capturing dependencies and context more effectively compared to traditional recurrent neural networks.

- Feed-Forward Neural Networks: The feed-forward neural networks within each layer of the encoder and decoder provide additional non-linear transformations to the sequence representations.

Let's understand how Transformer Networks work. The input sequence is first embedded into continuous vector representations, which allow the model to understand the semantics of the tokens. The input embeddings are passed through multiple encoder layers. Each encoder layer performs self-attention, allowing each position in the input sequence to attend to all other positions and compute an attention score based on their relevance to the current position.

After self-attention, the representations are passed through feed-forward neural networks, adding non-linearity and additional context. During the decoding process (in sequence-to-sequence tasks), the decoder attends to the previously generated positions in the output sequence using self-attention. Additionally, it can attend to the encoder's output to extract relevant information needed for decoding.

The decoder produces the output sequence step-by-step, generating one token at a time autoregressively. The process continues until the end-of-sequence token is generated.

Implementing a complete Transformer Network from scratch in Python can be quite complex. However, you can use popular deep learning libraries such as TensorFlow or PyTorch, which provide pre-built Transformer models and APIs to facilitate their use in various tasks like machine translation and language modelling. Let's take a high-level look at how to use a Transformer model using Hugging Face's "transformers" library in Python:

```python
# Install the transformers library (if not already installed)
# pip install transformers

import torch
from transformers import BertTokenizer, BertForMaskedLM

# Load pre-trained BERT model and tokenizer
tokenizer = BertTokenizer.from_pretrained('bert-base-uncased')
model = BertForMaskedLM.from_pretrained('bert-base-uncased')

# Input text for masked language modeling
text = "The quick brown [MASK] jumps over the lazy dog."

# Tokenize the input text
inputs = tokenizer(text, return_tensors="pt")

# Get the masked token index
masked_index = torch.where(inputs["input_ids"][0] == tokenizer.mask_token_id)

# Predict missing word using the pre-trained BERT model
with torch.no_grad():
    outputs = model(**inputs)
predictions = outputs.logits[0, masked_index, :]

# Get the top predicted tokens and their probabilities
top_predictions = torch.topk(predictions, k=5, dim=1)
predicted_tokens = tokenizer.convert_ids_to_tokens(top_predictions.indices[0])
predicted_probabilities = top_predictions.values[0]
```

```
# Print the top predicted tokens and their probabilities
for token, probability in zip(predicted_tokens, predicted_probabilities):
    print(f"{token}: {probability:.4f}")

cat: 9.9688
dog: 9.2704
bear: 8.8879
man: 8.7482
##ie: 8.5207
```

In this code, we load a pre-trained BERT (Bidirectional Encoder Representations from Transformers) model and tokenizer using Hugging Face's "transformers" library. BERT is a popular variant of Transformer Networks that has been pre-trained on a large corpus of text.

We input a sentence with a masked word (represented by [MASK]), tokenize it, and pass it through the pre-trained BERT model. The model predicts the most likely tokens to fill in the masked word, and we print the top predicted tokens and their probabilities.

Please note that the above example is a simplified demonstration of using a pre-trained Transformer model for masked language modelling. Implementing a complete Transformer architecture for more complex tasks like machine translation would involve additional components and considerations, such as the encoder-decoder structure and attention masks. The "transformers" library makes it easier to use pre-trained Transformer models for various natural language processing tasks, and it provides extensive documentation and examples for specific use cases.

Summary

In this chapter, we embarked on a journey through the world of neural networks, a fundamental component of modern deep learning systems. We explored various types of neural networks, each designed to tackle specific tasks and leverage the power of interconnected artificial neurons to mimic the human brain's computational abilities.

The chapter began by delving into the computational structure of neural networks. We learned that neural networks consist of layers of interconnected nodes, known as neurons or perceptrons. Next, we gained insights into how neural networks work. We learned that neural networks go through two primary phases: training and inference. The chapter then introduced the perceptron, a fundamental building block of neural networks.

Moving on, we delved into the concept of multi-layer perceptrons (MLPs), which are more powerful than single-layer perceptrons. We then explored convolutional neural networks (CNNs), a specialized type of neural network designed for image and video processing tasks. Recurrent neural networks (RNNs) were the next topic of exploration. Unlike feedforward networks, RNNs have feedback connections, allowing them to retain information from previous time steps. In the context of RNNs, we also discussed Long Short-Term Memory (LSTM) networks. LSTMs are a variant of RNNs that mitigate the vanishing gradient problem, enabling them to capture long-range dependencies in sequential data more effectively.

Furthermore, we delved into Generative Adversarial Networks (GANs), an exciting class of neural networks for generating synthetic data. GANs consist of two networks, a generator and a discriminator, which engage in a competitive process. Finally, we explored Transformer networks, a revolutionary architecture that has revolutionized natural language processing.

Chapter 12: Exploring Time Series Forecasting Algorithms

Introduction

Time Series Forecasting is a subfield of predictive analytics that focuses on predicting future values based on past observations in chronological order. It involves analyzing and modelling data points collected over time to make predictions about future trends, patterns, or behaviour. Time series forecasting is commonly used in various industries, including finance, economics, weather forecasting, sales, and resource planning.

Time Series Forecasting algorithms are applied to Time Series Data. Time Series Data is a type of data where observations are recorded at successive time intervals. Each data point is associated with a specific timestamp, and the sequence of data points represents a temporal order. Time series data often exhibit trends, seasonality, and other patterns that can be leveraged for forecasting future values.

Time Series Forecasting plays a crucial role in decision-making and planning for businesses and organizations. By accurately predicting future trends and patterns, businesses can anticipate demand, manage resources efficiently, optimize inventory, and make informed strategic decisions. Time series forecasting is used in financial markets to predict stock prices and currency exchange rates, in retail for sales forecasting, in weather forecasting to predict temperature, precipitation, and other meteorological variables, and in numerous other domains to enhance operational efficiency and optimize outcomes.

One real-time business problem where time series forecasting is employed is sales forecasting for retail businesses. Retailers need to accurately predict future sales to ensure sufficient inventory levels, plan promotional activities, and optimize staffing and logistics. By analyzing historical sales data and using time series forecasting models, retailers can anticipate fluctuations in demand, identify seasonal patterns, and adjust their operations accordingly. For example, a retail store can use time series forecasting to predict sales for the upcoming holiday season and strategically plan its marketing campaigns and inventory stocking to meet customer demands efficiently.

Another example is energy consumption forecasting for utility companies. Electric utility providers need to forecast future energy demand to ensure a stable and reliable supply of electricity. By using historical energy consumption data and incorporating factors like weather patterns and seasonal variations, time series forecasting models can predict future energy demand accurately. This enables utility companies to optimize power generation, plan maintenance activities, and manage their energy resources effectively.

In both examples, time series forecasting empowers businesses and organizations with valuable insights to make data-driven decisions, improve operational efficiency, and stay ahead of the competition in dynamic and unpredictable environments.

Getting Started with ARIMA for Time Series Forecasting

ARIMA (AutoRegressive Integrated Moving Average) is a popular time series forecasting model that combines autoregression, differencing, and moving average components to make predictions about future values based on past observations. ARIMA models are widely used in various domains, such as economics, finance, and meteorology, to forecast trends and patterns in time series data.

The mathematical formula of ARIMA(p, d, q) can be expressed as follows:

ARIMA(p, d, q):

$$Y_t = c + \sum_{i=1}^{p} \phi_i Y_{t-i} + \sum_{i=1}^{q} \theta_i \epsilon_{t-i} + \epsilon_t$$

Here:

- Y_t is the value of the time series at time t
- c is the constant term
- ϕ_i are the autoregressive coefficients
- θ_i are the moving average coefficients
- ϵ_t is the white noise error term

The ARIMA model is based on three fundamental principles:

- AutoRegression (AR): It models the relationship between the current value and its past values (lagged values) in the time series data.

- Integration (I): It handles the issue of non-stationarity by differencing the time series data to make it stationary. Stationarity implies that the mean and variance of the time series remain constant over time.

- Moving Average (MA): It models the relationship between the current value and past error terms (residuals) in the time series data.

Before applying ARIMA, it is essential to ensure that the time series data is stationary, as ARIMA assumes stationarity. Stationarity can be assessed using statistical tests or visual inspection of the data. If the data is non-stationary (i.e., exhibits trends or seasonality), differencing is applied to transform the data to achieve stationarity. Differencing involves computing the difference between consecutive observations at a certain lag (usually 1) to remove trends and make the time series stationary.

Below are examples of stationary and non-stationary time series data:

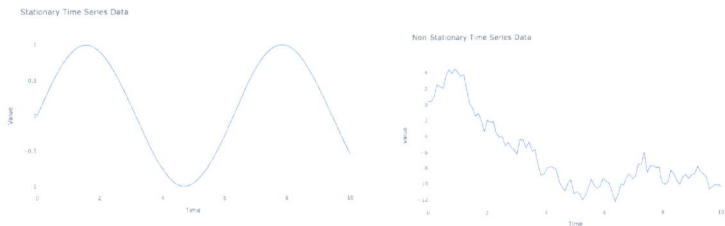

Selecting appropriate values for the p, d, and q parameters is critical for building an effective ARIMA model. This process involves analyzing the autocorrelation and partial autocorrelation plots of the time series data to identify the appropriate values for p and q. The value of d is determined based on the number of differencing steps needed to achieve stationarity. Generally, if the data is stationary, the value of d is 0, and if the data is not stationary, the value of d is 1.

Implementing ARIMA models in Python can be done using libraries like statsmodels or pandas. Statsmodels provides a comprehensive set of tools for time series analysis, including ARIMA modelling. Below is a simplified example of implementing ARIMA using statsmodels on my Instagram reach data (you can download the data from the link below:

Dataset link: statso.io/social-media-reach-forecasting-case-study/

```python
# Importing Necessay Python libraries
import pandas as pd
import numpy as np
import matplotlib.pyplot as plt
import plotly.graph_objs as go
import plotly.express as px
import plotly.io as pio
pio.templates.default = "plotly_white"
from statsmodels.tsa.arima.model import ARIMA
from statsmodels.graphics.tsaplots import plot_acf, plot_pacf
```

Here we are just importing the necessary Python libraries required for the task of Time Series Forecasting using ARIMA. Now let's read the data:

```python
# reading the data
data = pd.read_csv('Instagram-Reach.csv')
print(data.head())
```

```
                    Date  Instagram reach
0  2022-04-01T00:00:00             7620
1  2022-04-02T00:00:00            12859
2  2022-04-03T00:00:00            16008
3  2022-04-04T00:00:00            24349
4  2022-04-05T00:00:00            20532
```

Now, we will extract only date values from the date column:

```python
# extracting only date values from the date cloumn

data["Date"] = pd.to_datetime(data["Date"])

# Extract only the date part from the "Date" column
data["Date"] = data["Date"].dt.date
```

Now let's visualize the trend of the data:

```python
# visualizing the trend of the data

fig = go.Figure()
fig.add_trace(go.Scatter(x=data['Date'],
                         y=data['Instagram reach'],
                         mode='lines', name='Instagram reach'))

fig.update_layout(title='Instagram Reach Trend', xaxis_title='Date',
                  yaxis_title='Instagram Reach')
```

```
fig.show()
```

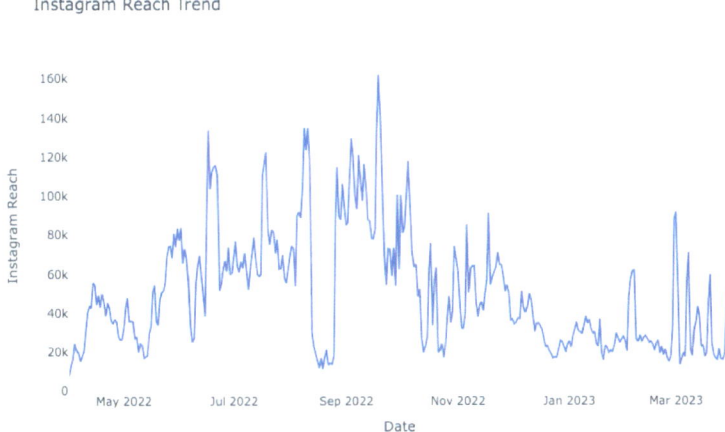

You can see that this data is not stationary, and it's not appropriate to use the ARIMA model on such data. On such data, we can use the SARIMA model, which we will explore later in the next section. For now, let's continue with the implementation of ARIMA on this dataset only:

```
# resetting index
time_series = data.set_index('Date')['Instagram reach']

# Differencing
differenced_series = time_series.diff().dropna()

# Plot ACF and PACF of differenced time series
fig, axes = plt.subplots(1, 2, figsize=(12, 4))
plot_acf(differenced_series, ax=axes[0])
plot_pacf(differenced_series, ax=axes[1])
plt.show()
```

Here we performed differencing and visualized the autocorrelation and partial autocorrelation plots which will help us in identifying the p and q values. Below is the output of the above code:

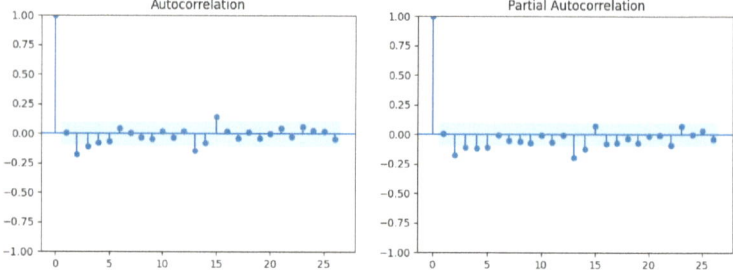

In the above graphs, we can see that the ACF plot cuts off at lag 1, indicating q=1. The PACF plot also cuts off at lag 1, indicating p=1. Now here's how to implement the ARIMA model to forecast time series:

```
p, d, q = 1, 1, 1 # d = 1 because the data is non-stationary
model = ARIMA(time_series, order=(p, d, q))
results = model.fit()

print(results.summary())
```

Now, here's how we can see the predicted values for the next 100 days:

```
# Predict future values
future_steps = 100
predictions = results.predict(len(time_series), len(time_series) + future_steps - 1)
```

```
2023-04-01    23434.362332
2023-04-02    24541.004432
2023-04-03    25403.218747
2023-04-04    26074.992871
2023-04-05    26598.389971
                  ...
2023-07-05    28444.663196
2023-07-06    28444.663196
2023-07-07    28444.663196
2023-07-08    28444.663196
2023-07-09    28444.663196
Freq: D, Name: predicted_mean, Length: 100, dtype: float64
```

ARIMA models have their strengths in simple linear time series forecasting, especially for short-term predictions and data with a well-defined temporal pattern. However, they may not be suitable for complex time series data with nonlinear trends or irregular seasonality, and their performance may be affected by data preprocessing requirements and the presence of outliers. Careful evaluation and consideration of the data characteristics are essential when deciding to use ARIMA models for time series forecasting.

SARIMA for Time Series Forecasting

SARIMA stands for Seasonal AutoRegressive Integrated Moving Average. It is an extension of the ARIMA model that incorporates seasonality in time series data. SARIMA is designed to handle time series data that exhibits periodic patterns or seasonal fluctuations over time. By considering seasonal effects, SARIMA models can provide more accurate forecasts for time series with repetitive seasonal behaviour.

The mathematical formula of SARIMA can be expressed as follows:

$$Y(t) = c + \phi_1 Y(t-1) + \phi_2 Y(t-2) + \ldots + \phi_p Y(t-p) + \theta_1 \varepsilon(t-1) + \theta_2 \varepsilon(t-2) + \ldots + \theta_p \varepsilon(t-q) + \varepsilon(t) + \Phi_1 Y(t-s) + \Phi_2 Y(t-2s) + \ldots + \Phi_p Y(t-Ps) + \Theta_1 \varepsilon(t-s) + \Theta_2 \varepsilon(t-2s) + \ldots + \Theta_p \varepsilon(t-Qs)$$

Here:

- $Y(t)$ is the value of the time series at time t.

- c is the constant or intercept term.

- p is the order of the autoregressive (AR) component, representing the number of lag observations included in the model.

- d is the order of differencing, representing the number of times the time series is differenced to make it stationary.

- q is the order of the moving average (MA) component, representing the number of lagged forecast errors in the model.

- ε(t) is the error term at time t.

- P is the seasonal order of the autoregressive (SAR) component, representing the number of seasonal lag observations included in the model.

- D is the seasonal order of differencing, representing the number of times the seasonal time series is differenced to make it stationary.

- Q is the seasonal order of the moving average (SMA) component, representing the number of seasonal lagged forecast errors in the model.

- s is the seasonal period, which represents the number of time steps per season (e.g., s=12 for monthly data with a yearly seasonality).

Time series data with seasonal patterns exhibit repetitive fluctuations or patterns at regular intervals. These seasonal effects can be daily, monthly, quarterly, or any other consistent time period. Seasonal patterns can be caused by factors like weather, holidays, or business cycles, and they can significantly impact the behaviour of the time series over time.

To implement the SARIMA model, we need to follow the same process we followed to implement the ARIMA model. Below are the changes you need to make in your implementation of ARIMA to implement the SARIMA model:

Import the SARIMAX class:

```
from statsmodels.tsa.statespace.sarimax import SARIMAX
```

And now to implement SARIMA, change your model from ARIMA to SARIMA and add seasonality parameters as shown in the code below:

```
p, d, q, s = 1, 1, 1, 12

model = SARIMAX(time_series, order=(p, d, q), seasonal_order=(p, d, q, s))
results = model.fit()
print(results.summary())
```

The value of s in SARIMA represents the seasonal period or the number of time steps in each seasonal cycle. In time series data, seasonality often occurs at regular intervals. For example, in monthly data, the seasonality repeats every 12 months, while in daily data, it may repeat every 7 days (weekly seasonality) or every 30 days (monthly seasonality).

In the provided SARIMA example, the value of s is set to 12, indicating that the time series data exhibits seasonality with a repeating pattern every 12 time steps. This typically corresponds to a seasonal cycle of 12 months, suggesting that the data has yearly seasonality.

SARIMA models offer advantages in accurately capturing seasonal patterns in time series data and providing reliable forecasts for seasonal fluctuations. However, their performance depends on correctly identifying the seasonal period and selecting appropriate model parameters. They may not be suitable for non-seasonal data, and model fitting can be computationally demanding for large datasets. Careful consideration and analysis of the data's seasonal behaviour are essential when deciding to use SARIMA for time series forecasting.

Summary

In this chapter, we delved into the world of Time Series Forecasting using two popular techniques: ARIMA (AutoRegressive Integrated Moving Average) and SARIMA (Seasonal AutoRegressive Integrated Moving Average). Time Series Forecasting is a crucial field in data analysis, where the goal is to predict future values based on past observations of a time-dependent dataset.

ARIMA and SARIMA are valuable tools in Time Series Forecasting, each with its strengths and limitations. By mastering these techniques, analysts and data scientists can make informed decisions and generate meaningful predictions for a wide range of real-world applications, including finance, sales forecasting, and demand prediction, among others. However, choosing the right model and understanding the data's characteristics are crucial steps in leveraging the full potential of these forecasting methods.

Appendix: All Parameters of Commonly Used Machine Learning Algorithms

Linear Regression:

The Linear Regression algorithm is implemented through the LinearRegression class. The main parameters of the Linear Regression algorithm are:

- **fit_intercept:** This parameter is a boolean flag that determines whether to calculate the intercept for the model. If set to True, the algorithm will estimate the intercept b0 of the linear equation. If set to False, the intercept will be assumed to be zero.

- **normalize:** This parameter is also a boolean flag that determines whether to normalize the input features before fitting the model. If set to True, the input features will be scaled to have zero mean and unit variance. Normalizing the features can be beneficial when they have significantly different scales.

- **copy_X:** This parameter is used to indicate whether the input data should be copied or not. If set to True, a copy of the input data will be made before fitting the model. If set to False, the model may modify the input data in place.

Polynomial Regression:

Polynomial Regression is implemented using the PolynomialFeatures class for feature engineering and the LinearRegression class for building the regression model. The main parameter for Polynomial Regression is:

- **degree:** This parameter specifies the degree of the polynomial features to be generated. It determines the highest power of the input features in the polynomial equation. For example, if degree=2, the polynomial features will include all combinations of the original features up to the second degree (quadratic features).

In addition to the degree parameter, the Linear Regression model used in Polynomial Regression has the same parameters as discussed earlier, such as fit_intercept, normalize, and copy_X.

Ridge Regression:

Ridge Regression is implemented through the Ridge class, which is a linear regression model with L2 regularization. The main parameter for Ridge Regression is:

- **alpha:** This parameter controls the strength of the L2 regularization term in the Ridge Regression model. It is a positive value that determines how much the model penalizes large coefficients. A higher value of alpha leads to stronger regularization, which helps in reducing overfitting.

In addition to the alpha parameter, the Ridge Regression model has the same parameters as the Linear Regression model, such as fit_intercept, normalize, and copy_X.

Lasso Regression:

Lasso Regression is implemented through the Lasso class, which is a linear regression model with L1 regularization. The main parameter for Lasso Regression is:

- **alpha:** This parameter controls the strength of the L1 regularization term in the Lasso Regression model. It is a positive value that determines how much the model penalizes the absolute values of the coefficients. A higher value of alpha leads to stronger regularization, encouraging some coefficients to become exactly zero, effectively performing feature selection.

In addition to the alpha parameter, the Lasso Regression model has the same parameters as the Linear Regression model, such as fit_intercept, normalize, and copy_X.

Elastic Net Regression:

Elastic Net Regression is implemented through the ElasticNet class, which is a linear regression model with a combination of L1 and L2 regularization. The main parameters for Elastic Net Regression are:

- **alpha:** This parameter controls the overall strength of the regularization term in the Elastic Net model. It is a positive value that determines the trade-off between L1 (Lasso) and

L2 (Ridge) regularization. A higher value of alpha results in stronger regularization, encouraging sparsity in the model.

- **l1_ratio:** This parameter controls the mix between L1 and L2 regularization in the Elastic Net model. It is a value between 0 and 1, where 0 corresponds to L2 regularization only (Ridge), 1 corresponds to L1 regularization only (Lasso), and values in between correspond to a mix of L1 and L2 regularization. The optimal value of l1_ratio depends on the dataset and the desired level of sparsity and feature selection.

In addition to the alpha and l1_ratio parameters, the Elastic Net Regression model has the same parameters as the Linear Regression model, such as fit_intercept, normalize, and copy_X.

Logistic Regression:

Logistic Regression is implemented through the LogisticRegression class. The main parameters for Logistic Regression are:

- **penalty:** This parameter determines the type of regularization used in the model. It can take values 'l1', 'l2', 'elasticnet', or 'none'. 'l1' corresponds to L1 regularization (Lasso), 'l2' corresponds to L2 regularization (Ridge), and 'elasticnet' corresponds to a combination of L1 and L2 regularization (Elastic Net). 'none' means no regularization.

- **C:** This parameter controls the inverse of the regularization strength, where larger values of C correspond to weaker regularization. It is a positive value, and the optimal value of C depends on the dataset and the level of regularization required. Smaller values of C increase the regularization strength, which helps to prevent overfitting.

- **solver:** This parameter specifies the optimization algorithm used to fit the model. The choice of the solver affects the convergence speed and stability of the optimization process. Common values for solver include 'lbfgs', 'liblinear', 'sag', 'saga', and 'newton-cg'.

- **max_iter:** This parameter sets the maximum number of iterations for the solver to converge. If the solver does not converge within this number of iterations, it will terminate without finding the optimal solution.

Linear Discriminant Analysis:

Linear Discriminant Analysis (LDA) is implemented through the LinearDiscriminantAnalysis class. The main parameters for Linear Discriminant Analysis are:

- **solver:** This parameter specifies the solver used for eigenvalue decomposition. The choice of the solver can impact the computational efficiency and numerical stability of the algorithm. Common values for solver include 'svd' (singular value decomposition), 'lsqr' (least squares solution), and 'eigen' (eigenvalue decomposition).

- **shrinkage:** This parameter controls the shrinkage applied to the covariance matrix to improve its numerical stability and estimation accuracy. It can take values between 0 and 1. A value of 0 means no shrinkage, while a value of 1 means complete shrinkage (diagonal covariance matrix).

- **n_components:** This parameter specifies the number of components (discriminants) to be kept. It determines the dimensionality of the projected space for classification. If n_components is not set, it will be automatically chosen as min(n_classes - 1, n_features), where n_classes is the number of unique classes in the target variable.

Stochastic Gradient Descent Classifier:

The stochastic Gradient Descent (SGD) Classifier is implemented through the SGDClassifier class. The main parameters for the SGD Classifier are:

- **loss:** This parameter specifies the loss function to be optimized during training. The choice of the loss function depends on the type of classification problem. For binary classification, common values include 'hinge' for linear SVM, 'log' for logistic regression, and 'modified_huber' for smoothed hinge loss. For multiclass classification, 'log' is commonly used.

- **alpha:** This parameter controls the regularization strength in the model. It is a positive value that determines the amount of regularization applied to the model. A higher value of alpha leads to stronger regularization, which helps to prevent overfitting.

- **penalty:** This parameter determines the type of regularization used. It can take values 'l1', 'l2', 'elasticnet', or 'none'. 'l1' corresponds to L1 regularization (Lasso), 'l2' corresponds to L2 regularization (Ridge), and 'elasticnet' corresponds to a combination of L1 and L2 regularization (Elastic Net). 'none' means no regularization.

- **max_iter:** This parameter sets the maximum number of iterations for the solver to converge. If the solver does not converge within this number of iterations, it will terminate without finding the optimal solution.

- **learning_rate:** This parameter determines the learning rate schedule for updating the model's parameters during training. Common values include 'constant', 'optimal', 'invscaling', and 'adaptive'.

Naive Bayes:

Naive Bayes classifiers are implemented through several classes, including GaussianNB for Gaussian Naive Bayes, MultinomialNB for Multinomial Naive Bayes, and BernoulliNB for Bernoulli Naive Bayes. The main parameters for these Naive Bayes classifiers are:

- **alpha:** This parameter is specific to MultinomialNB and BernoulliNB and represents the additive (Laplace/Lidstone) smoothing parameter. It is a non-negative value, and a value of 0 means no smoothing is applied. The optimal value of alpha depends on the dataset and the level of smoothing required.

- **var_smoothing:** This parameter is specific to GaussianNB and represents the portion of the largest variance of all features added to variances for calculation stability. It is a non-negative value, and a small value close to zero is typically used for numerical stability.

When implementing Naive Bayes classifiers using scikit-learn, the choice of the optimal value for alpha or var_smoothing depends on the nature of the data and the problem. For MultinomialNB and

BernoulliNB, alpha is usually set to a small value, such as 1.0 or smaller, to perform Laplace smoothing and handle cases where some features have zero probabilities. For GaussianNB, var_smoothing is typically set to a small value close to zero.

Support Vector Machines:

Support Vector Machines (SVM) are implemented through the SVC class for classification and SVR class for regression. The main parameters for SVM are:

- **C:** This parameter controls the regularization strength, where larger values of C correspond to weaker regularization. It is a positive value, and the optimal value of C depends on the dataset and the level of regularization required. Smaller values of C increase the regularization strength, which helps to prevent overfitting.

- **kernel:** This parameter specifies the type of kernel function used to transform the input data into a higher-dimensional space. Common kernel functions include 'linear', 'poly', 'rbf' (radial basis function), and 'sigmoid'. The choice of the kernel depends on the linearity of the data and the complexity of the decision boundary.

- **gamma:** This parameter is specific to 'rbf', 'poly', and 'sigmoid' kernels and controls the influence of a single training example on the decision boundary. It is a positive value, and smaller values of gamma lead to a smoother decision boundary, while larger values make the decision boundary more flexible.

- **degree:** This parameter is specific to 'poly' kernel and sets the degree of the polynomial used in the kernel function. Higher values of degree allow the model to fit more complex data, but they can also lead to overfitting.

- **epsilon:** This parameter is specific to SVR and sets the epsilon-tube within which no penalty is associated with errors. It controls the width of the tube around the regression line within which errors are ignored.

When implementing SVM using scikit-learn, the optimal range of values for the C, gamma, and degree parameters depends on the dataset and the complexity of the problem. It is common to use a logarithmic scale for C and gamma, trying values that span several orders of magnitude. For degree, values typically range from 1 to 5 or higher depending on the complexity of the data.

Decision Trees:

Decision Trees are implemented through the DecisionTreeClassifier class for classification and DecisionTreeRegressor class for regression. The main parameters for Decision Trees are:

- **criterion:** This parameter specifies the criterion used to measure the quality of a split. For classification tasks, 'gini' is used for Gini impurity, and 'entropy' is used for information gain. For regression tasks, 'mse' (mean squared error) and 'mae' (mean absolute error) are commonly used.

- **splitter:** This parameter determines the strategy used to choose the split at each node. The options are 'best' to choose the best split and 'random' to choose the best random split. The 'best' option is the default for Decision Trees.

- **max_depth:** This parameter controls the maximum depth of the tree. It restricts the depth of the decision tree and helps prevent overfitting. If not specified, the tree will be expanded until all leaves are pure or contain fewer samples than min_samples_split.

- **min_samples_split:** This parameter sets the minimum number of samples required to split an internal node. If a node has fewer samples than min_samples_split, it will not be split further. This parameter helps control the growth of the tree.

- **min_samples_leaf:** This parameter sets the minimum number of samples required to be at a leaf node. If a leaf node has fewer samples than min_samples_leaf, it may be pruned to avoid overfitting.

- **max_features:** This parameter determines the maximum number of features to consider when looking for the best split. It can take various values, such as 'auto' (sqrt(n_features)), 'sqrt' (same as 'auto'), 'log2' (log2(n_features)), or an integer value. A smaller value can reduce overfitting.

When implementing Decision Trees using scikit-learn, finding the optimal range of values for max_depth, min_samples_split, min_samples_leaf, and max_features is essential to avoid overfitting and achieve good generalization performance. The optimal range of values for these parameters will depend on the complexity of the dataset and the size of the training data.

Random Forests:

Random Forest is implemented through the RandomForestClassifier class for classification and RandomForestRegressor class for regression. The main parameters for Random Forest are:

- **n_estimators:** This parameter specifies the number of trees in the forest. Increasing the number of trees generally improves the model's performance, up to a certain point. Common values for n_estimators range from 10 to 100 or more.

- **criterion:** This parameter specifies the criterion used to measure the quality of a split in each tree. For classification tasks, 'gini' is used for Gini impurity, and 'entropy' is used for information gain. For regression tasks, 'mse' (mean squared error) and 'mae' (mean absolute error) are commonly used.

- **max_depth:** This parameter controls the maximum depth of the trees in the forest. It restricts the depth of each decision tree and helps prevent overfitting. If not specified, the trees will be expanded until all leaves are pure or contain fewer samples than min_samples_split.

- **min_samples_split:** This parameter sets the minimum number of samples required to split an internal node. If a node has fewer samples than min_samples_split, it will not be split further. This parameter helps control the growth of individual trees.

- **min_samples_leaf:** This parameter sets the minimum number of samples required to be at a leaf node. If a leaf node has fewer samples than min_samples_leaf, it may be pruned to avoid overfitting.

- **max_features:** This parameter determines the maximum number of features to consider when looking for the best split in each tree. It can take various values, such as 'auto' (sqrt(n_features)), 'sqrt' (same as 'auto'), 'log2' (log2(n_features)), or an integer value. A smaller value can reduce overfitting.

- **bootstrap:** This parameter controls whether bootstrap samples are used when building trees. If set to True (default), each tree is built on a random subset of the training data (with replacement). If set to False, the entire training dataset is used to build each tree.

- **random_state:** This parameter is used to seed the random number generator, ensuring reproducibility of results.

When implementing Random Forest using scikit-learn, finding the optimal range of values for n_estimators, max_depth, min_samples_split, min_samples_leaf, and max_features is essential to achieve good generalization performance and avoiding overfitting. The optimal range of values for these parameters will depend on the complexity of the dataset and the size of the training data.

Gradient Boosting:

Gradient Boosting is implemented through the GradientBoostingClassifier class for classification and GradientBoostingRegressor class for regression. The main parameters for Gradient Boosting are:

- **n_estimators:** This parameter specifies the number of boosting stages (trees) to be built. Increasing the number of estimators can improve the model's performance, but it also increases the computational cost. Common values for n_estimators range from 50 to 500 or more.

- **learning_rate:** This parameter controls the contribution of each tree to the final prediction. A smaller learning rate requires more estimators to achieve the same level of accuracy. Typical values for learning_rate are 0.01, 0.1, or 0.3.

- **max_depth:** This parameter controls the maximum depth of the individual trees. Setting a small value for max_depth can prevent overfitting, but it may also lead to underfitting. Common values for max_depth are around 3 to 10.

- **min_samples_split:** This parameter sets the minimum number of samples required to split an internal node. If a node has fewer samples than min_samples_split, it will not be split further. This parameter helps control the growth of individual trees and can be set to an integer value or a float representing the fraction of total samples.

- **min_samples_leaf:** This parameter sets the minimum number of samples required to be at a leaf node. If a leaf node has fewer samples than min_samples_leaf, it may be pruned to avoid overfitting.

- **max_features:** This parameter determines the maximum number of features to consider when looking for the best split in each tree. It can take various values, such as 'auto' (sqrt(n_features)), 'sqrt' (same as 'auto'), 'log2' (log2(n_features)), or an integer value. A smaller value can reduce overfitting.

- **subsample:** This parameter controls the fraction of samples used for fitting the individual trees. Values less than 1.0 allow for stochastic gradient boosting, which can help improve generalization. Common values for subsample are 0.8 or 0.9.

- **loss:** This parameter specifies the loss function to be optimized. For classification tasks, 'deviance' is used for logistic regression, and 'exponential' is used for AdaBoost. For regression tasks, 'ls' (least squares) and 'lad' (least absolute deviation) are commonly used.

When implementing Gradient Boosting using scikit-learn, finding the optimal range of values for n_estimators, learning_rate, max_depth, min_samples_split, min_samples_leaf, max_features, and subsample is important to achieve good generalization performance and avoid overfitting. The optimal range of values for these parameters will depend on the complexity of the dataset and the size of the training data.

K-Means:

K-means clustering is implemented through the KMeans class. The main parameters for K-means clustering are:

- **n_clusters:** This parameter specifies the number of clusters to be formed. It represents the value of 'k' in K-means. It is essential to choose an appropriate number of clusters to obtain meaningful results. The optimal value of n_clusters depends on the data and the problem domain. There are various methods to determine the optimal number of clusters, such as the elbow method, silhouette score, or using domain knowledge.

- **init:** This parameter determines the method for initializing the cluster centroids. The 'k-means++' method is the default, which selects initial centroids to be distant from each other, leading to faster convergence and better results in most cases. Other options include 'random', which randomly selects initial centroids from data points, and providing an array of initial centroids.

- **n_init:** This parameter controls the number of times the K-means algorithm will be run with different centroid seeds. The final result will be the best output among n_init runs in terms of inertia (sum of squared distances from samples to their closest cluster center). A higher value of n_init increases the chances of finding a globally optimal solution but also increases computation time.

- **max_iter:** This parameter sets the maximum number of iterations for the K-means algorithm to converge to a solution. If the algorithm does not converge within max_iter iterations, it will stop and return the current result. Convergence typically occurs much before reaching max_iter, especially for well-behaved datasets.

- **tol:** This parameter sets the tolerance for convergence. If the change in the inertia (sum of squared distances from samples to their closest cluster center) between two consecutive iterations is less than tol, the algorithm is considered to have converged, and the optimization stops.

- **random_state:** This parameter is used to seed the random number generator, ensuring reproducibility of results.

When implementing K-means clustering using scikit-learn, choosing the optimal value for n_clusters is essential for meaningful cluster assignments. As mentioned earlier, there are various methods to determine the optimal number of clusters, and it may require experimentation and analysis of the data.

DBSCAN:

DBSCAN (Density-Based Spatial Clustering of Applications with Noise) is implemented through the DBSCAN class. The main parameters for DBSCAN clustering are:

- **eps:** This parameter represents the maximum distance between two samples for one to be considered as in the neighbourhood of the other. It defines the radius of the neighbourhood around each data point. A smaller value of eps means tighter clusters, while a larger value means larger clusters.

- **min_samples:** This parameter sets the minimum number of samples (data points) in a neighbourhood to consider a point as a core point. Core points are the central points of a cluster, and they must have at least min_samples points in their neighbourhood (including the point itself) to form a cluster. Points that are not core points but are within the neighbourhood of a core point are considered border points and are part of the same cluster as the core point.

- **metric:** This parameter specifies the distance metric used to measure the distance between data points. Common distance metrics include 'euclidean' (Euclidean distance), 'manhattan' (Manhattan distance), 'cosine' (cosine similarity), and others. The choice of the metric depends on the nature of the data and the problem.

- **algorithm:** This parameter determines the algorithm used to compute the nearest neighbours. The default is 'auto', which automatically chooses the best algorithm based on the data and other parameters. Other options include 'ball_tree', 'kd_tree', and 'brute'.

- **leaf_size:** This parameter is relevant when using the 'ball_tree' or 'kd_tree' algorithm for computing nearest neighbors. It sets the size of the leaf nodes in the tree data structure, affecting the speed and memory consumption.

- **p:** This parameter is relevant when using the 'minkowski' distance metric. It specifies the power parameter for the Minkowski distance calculation. When p=1, it is equivalent to using the 'manhattan' distance, and when p=2, it is equivalent to using the 'euclidean' distance.

When implementing DBSCAN using scikit-learn, choosing the optimal values for eps and min_samples is crucial to obtain meaningful clusters. The optimal values depend on the density and distribution of the data points. It is often recommended to perform parameter tuning using techniques like grid search or cross-validation to find the best combination of eps and min_samples.

Convolutional Neural Networks:

Convolutional Neural Networks (CNNs) are implemented through the Sequential class for creating a sequential model or the Model class for more complex architectures. The main parameters for CNNs in Keras include:

- **Convolutional Layers:** The number of convolutional layers and their configurations, such as the number of filters (or kernels), the size of the filters, and the padding method.

- **Pooling Layers:** The number of pooling layers and their configurations, such as the pooling type (e.g., max pooling or average pooling) and the pool size.

- **Activation Functions:** The choice of activation functions for hidden layers and the output layer. Common choices include 'relu', 'sigmoid', 'tanh', and 'softmax'.

- **Dropout:** The dropout rate, if used, to prevent overfitting. The dropout rate typically ranges from 0.2 to 0.5.

- **Optimizer:** The optimization algorithm used to update the model's weights during training. Popular optimizers include 'adam', 'sgd' (stochastic gradient descent), and 'rmsprop'.

- **Learning Rate:** The learning rate of the optimizer, which controls the step size in weight updates during training. Typical values range from 0.001 to 0.1.

- **Batch Size:** The number of samples used in each training update. Larger batch sizes may lead to more stable training but require more memory.

- **Number of Epochs:** The number of times the model will iterate over the entire training dataset during training.

- **Loss Function:** The loss function to be minimized during training. For classification problems, 'binary_crossentropy' is commonly used for binary classification, and 'categorical_crossentropy' is used for multi-class classification.

- **Metrics:** The evaluation metrics used during training and testing, such as 'accuracy', 'precision', 'recall', or 'F1-score'.

Recurrent Neural Networks:

Recurrent Neural Networks (RNNs) are implemented through the Sequential class or the Model class for more complex architectures. The main parameters for RNNs in Keras include:

- **Number of Units:** The number of units or neurons in the RNN layer. This parameter determines the capacity of the RNN to learn complex patterns in the sequence data. A larger number of units allows the RNN to capture more intricate patterns but also increases computational complexity.

- **Activation Function:** The choice of activation function for the RNN layer. Common choices include 'tanh', 'relu', and 'sigmoid'. The activation function introduces non-linearity in the RNN layer, enabling it to learn complex relationships in sequential data.

- **Return Sequences:** A Boolean parameter that indicates whether the RNN layer should return the entire sequence of outputs for each time step or only the final output. For many-to-one sequence prediction tasks, setting return_sequences=False is typical.

- **Input Shape:** The shape of the input data, which includes the number of time steps and features for each input sequence. The input shape depends on the nature of the sequence data.

- **Batch Size:** The number of input sequences used in each training update. Larger batch sizes may lead to more stable training but require more memory.

- **Number of Epochs:** The number of times the model will iterate over the entire training dataset during training.

- **Loss Function:** The loss function to be minimized during training. For sequential data and time series prediction, appropriate loss functions may include 'mean_squared_error', 'mean_absolute_error', or custom-defined loss functions.

- **Optimizer:** The optimization algorithm used to update the model's weights during training. Common optimizers include 'adam', 'rmsprop', and 'sgd'.

- **Learning Rate:** The learning rate of the optimizer, which controls the step size in weight updates during training. Typical values range from 0.001 to 0.1.

- **Dropout:** The dropout rate, if used, to prevent overfitting. The dropout rate typically ranges from 0.2 to 0.5.

Final Words - From the Author

Congratulations! You've reached the end of "Machine Learning Algorithms: Handbook," a comprehensive journey through the fundamental algorithms and techniques that power modern machine learning. Throughout this book, you have gained valuable insights into regression, classification, clustering, deep learning, and more. Armed with this knowledge, you are now equipped to tackle a wide range of real-world problems and unleash the true potential of machine learning.

Remember that machine learning is a continuously evolving field, and staying up-to-date with the latest advancements is crucial. As you venture into your machine learning endeavours beyond this handbook, here are some recommended next steps to maximize the utility of what you've learned:

- **Practice on Real-world Datasets:** To truly grasp the nuances of machine learning algorithms, work on various real-world datasets. Explore Statso.io/community, Kaggle, UCI Machine Learning Repository, or Google's TensorFlow datasets. Engaging with diverse datasets will broaden your understanding of different problem domains and data characteristics.

- **Implement Projects:** The best way to solidify your understanding is to implement machine learning algorithms to solve problems in your projects. Start with simple projects and gradually move to more complex ones. By doing so, you'll encounter real challenges that require thoughtful data preprocessing, algorithm selection, and performance evaluation.

- **Collaborate and Participate:** Join machine learning communities, and forums, and attend workshops or conferences if possible. Collaborating with like-minded individuals and learning from others' experiences can offer valuable insights and feedback. Sharing your knowledge and helping others in the community can also be a great way to reinforce your understanding.

- **Stay Updated with Research Papers:** Subscribe to academic journals, and follow researchers and Creators based on Data Science and Machine Learning on platforms like Google Scholar, LinkedIn, and Instagram. Regularly reading research papers will keep you abreast of cutting-edge algorithms and advancements in the field.

- **Experiment with Hyperparameters:** Dive into the Appendix section of this book to access all the parameters of commonly used machine learning algorithms. Experiment with tuning these hyperparameters to optimize your models' performance. Hyperparameter tuning is an essential skill in machine learning.

- **Explore Specialized Topics:** Delve deeper into specific subfields of machine learning that interest you the most. This could include natural language processing, computer vision, reinforcement learning, or any other niche area that aligns with your passion and career goals.

- **Consider Online Courses and Certifications:** If you wish to formalize your machine learning education, consider enrolling in online courses or certification programs offered by reputable platforms like Coursera, Udemy, or edX. These courses often provide hands-on projects and industry-relevant content.

- **Build a Portfolio:** As you work on various projects, keep a record of your work and showcase your best models on platforms like GitHub or personal blogs like Medium. A strong portfolio can impress potential employers or collaborators and open new opportunities in the machine learning field.

Feel free to give me a review of this book. Below are some of the platforms where you can find me:

- Amankharwal.official on Instagram
- Aman Kharwal on LinkedIn

Thanks!

Milton Keynes UK
Ingram Content Group UK Ltd.
UKHW021201210624
444479UK00001B/2